FOREWORD

This anthology, which includes all the poems prescribed for the Ordinary Level English Leaving Certificate Examinations of 2008, has been prepared by three experienced teachers of English. Each of the contributors has been able to concentrate on a limited number of the prescribed poets and their work, thus facilitating a high standard of research and presentation.

Guidelines are given which set each poem in context. In addition, each poem is accompanied by a glossary and appropriate explorations, designed to allow the student to find his/her authentic response to the material. Relevant biographical details are provided for each poet.

Guidelines are included for students on approaching the Unseen Poetry section of the course. There is also advice on approaching the prescribed question in the examination. Students will also find the glossary of poetic terms a valuable resource in reading and responding to poetry.

The poetry course for Leaving Certificate English demands a personal and active engagement from the student reader. We hope that this anthology makes that engagement possible and encourages students to explore the wider world of poetry for themselves. Due to the poet's wishes, we have not included guidelines or questions with the poetry of Adrienne Rich.

CONTENTS

newdiscovery

**Leaving Certificate Poetry Anthology
for Ordinary Level 2008**

Patrick Murray
Kevin McDermott
Mary Slattery

First published 2006

The Educational Company
Ballymount Road
Walkinstown
Dublin 12

A member of the Smurfit Kappa Group

Editor: Stephanie Dagg
Design and layout: Identikit
Cover photograph: Getty Images
Printed in Ireland by Future Print Ltd.

0 1 2 3 4 5 6 7 8 9

AEN 54815

CAROL ANN DUFFY

PAUL DURCAN

ROBERT FROST

KERRY HARDIE

ROGER MCGOUGH

JOHN MONTAGUE

PAUL MULDOON

RICHARD MURPHY

SHARON OLDS

PERCY BYSSHE SHELLEY

RICHARD WILBUR

ACKNOWLEDGEMENTS

The poems in this book have been reproduced with the kind permission of their publishers, agents, authors or their estates as follows;

'Phenomenal Woman' by Maya Angelou from *And Still I Rise* (1978) published by Virago Press, reproduced by kind permission of Random House Inc.

'It Ain't What You Do It's What It Does To You' by Simon Armitage from *Zoom!* (Bloodaxe Books, 1989)

'Child of Our Time' and 'This Moment' from *Collected Poems* (1995) by Eavan Boland, published by Carcanet Press Limited.

'Valentine' by Carol Ann Duffy from *Mean Time* (1993) published by Anvil Press Poetry

'Going Home to Mayo' by Paul Durcan by kind permission of the poet

'"Out, out—"', 'Spring Pools', 'Acquainted with the Night' and 'The Road Not Taken' by Robert Frost from *The Poetry of Robert Frost* edited by Edward Conner Lathaem, Copyright 1928, 1969 by Henry Holt and Company, Copyright 1936, 1942, 1956 by Robert Frost, Copyright 1964, 1970 by Lesley Frost Ballantine. Reprinted by permission of Henry Holt and Company, LLC

'May' by Kerry Hardie from *A Furious Place* (1996) by kind permission of the author and The Gallery Press, Loughcrew, Oldcastle, Co. Meath

'Postscript' by Seamus Heaney from *The Spirit Level* (1996) published by Faber and Faber Ltd

'The Ladybird's Story' by Elizabeth Jennings published by kind permission of David Higham Associates Ltd

'At Grass' from *The Less Deceived* (1955), 'An Arundel Tomb' from *The Whitsun Weddings* (1964), 'The Explosion' from *High Windows* (1974) by Philip Larkin, all published by Faber and Faber Ltd

'After The Titanic', 'Grandfather', 'Antarctica' by Derek Mahon from *Collected Poems* (1999) by kind permission of the author and The Gallery Press, Loughcrew, Oldcastle, Co. Meath

'Bearhugs' by Roger McGough from *Defying Gravity* (1993) published by Penguin Books reproduced by kind permission of Peters Fraser Dunlop Ltd

MAYA
ANGELOU

B. 1928

BIOGRAPHY

Maya Angelou was born on April 4, 1928 in St Louis, Missouri, USA. She grew up in segregated rural Arkansas. She is a writer, actress, playwright, civil-rights activist, producer and director. She lectures throughout the USA and abroad and has been Reynolds Professor of American Studies at Wake Forest University in North Carolina since 1981.

Maya Angelou began her career in drama and dance. She married a South African freedom fighter and lived in Cairo where she was editor of *The Arab Observer*, the only English-language news weekly in the Middle East. In Ghana, she was features editor of the African review and taught at the University of Ghana. In the 1960s, at the request of Dr Martin Luther King Jr, Angelou became the northern coordinator for the Southern Christian Leadership Conference. In 1993 she read one of her poems at the inauguration of President Bill Clinton.

Her account of her traumatic childhood and youth, *I Know Why the Caged Bird Sings*, became a bestselling book, as well as achieving critical acclaim in the 1970s. She has written and produced several prize-winning documentaries and screenplays. In theatre, she has produced, directed and acted in many plays. Her performance of her own poetry is highly entertaining and popular.

PHENOMENAL WOMAN

Pretty women wonder where my secret lies.
I'm not cute or built to suit a fashion model's size
But when I start to tell them,
They think I'm telling lies.
I say,   5
It's in the reach of my arms
The span of my hips,
The stride of my step,
The curl of my lips.
I'm a woman   10
Phenomenally.
Phenomenal woman,
That's me.
I walk into a room
Just as cool as you please,   15
And to a man,
The fellows stand or
Fall down on their knees.
Then they swarm around me,
A hive of honey bees.   20
I say,
It's the fire in my eyes,
And the flash of my teeth,
The swing in my waist,
And the joy in my feet.   25
I'm a woman
Phenomenally.
Phenomenal woman,
That's me.
Men themselves have wondered   30
What they see in me.
They try so much
But they can't touch
My inner mystery.

When I try to show them,   35
They say they still can't see.
I say,
It's in the arch of my back,
The sun of my smile,
The ride of my breasts,   40
The grace of my style.
I'm a woman
Phenomenally.
Phenomenal woman,
That's me.   45
Now you understand
Just why my head's not bowed.
I don't shout or jump about
Or have to talk real loud.
When you see me passing   50
It ought to make you proud.
I say,
It's in the click of my heels,
The bend of my hair,
The palm of my hand,   55
The need for my care,
'Cause I'm a woman
Phenomenally.
Phenomenal woman,
That's me.   60

GLOSSARY

title *Phenomenal*: extraordinary

GUIDELINES

The title says almost everything about the theme and feeling in the poem. The speaker is full of pride and confidence in herself, although, as she suggests, she may not be 'pretty' in a conventional sense. Her confidence arises from her ease with her own body. People react positively to her, she tells us, particularly men, like bees to honey. By repeating the words 'phenomenally' and 'phenomenal' she makes sure the reader gets the point!

But she also suggests that her attraction goes beyond the physical. Its source is in her 'inner mystery', which is connected with being a woman but also with her personality – how she smiles, her sense of style.

In the final section of the poem, she says that she feels people should be proud to see her passing by, just because she is who she is, a 'phenomenal' woman, not just someone looking for attention. There is an indirect reference here to the difficulties she has had to overcome in her life, as an emotionally damaged and abused child whose head you might expect to be 'bowed', or defeated by her experiences. This woman is not prepared to let her past determine how she feels in the present, as the final lines make clear.

QUESTIONS

1 How does the speaker suggest that she is not like other 'pretty women'?
2 How do the physical images help to convey the theme of the poem?
3 What sort of woman is the speaker of the poem, in your view?
4 Would you agree that there is a tremendous sense of energy in the poem? How is it created?
5 Do you think you would like this woman, if you met her?
6 Maya Angelou has performed this poem on the stage. Even if you have not seen it, or a televised version, try to describe how you think she may have done so.
7 Do you think this poem has anything to teach people, both men and women? If so, can you say what it might be?
8 Write a short note to Maya Angelou describing your response to her poem.

SIMON ARMITAGE

B. 1963

BIOGRAPHY

Simon Armitage was born in 1963 in Huddersfield and grew up in West Yorkshire. He studied geography at Portsmouth Polytechnic and later social work and psychology at Manchester University. He has worked as a shelf stacker, disc jockey and lathe operator. For some time he worked as a probation officer. He is now a freelance writer.

He has presented poetry programmes for the BBC, worked as an editor and taught at the University of Leeds and the University of Iowa, USA. In 2000 he was writer-in-residence at the Millennium Dome in London.

Armitage is the author of nine volumes of poetry, including *Zoom!* (1989), *Kid* (1992) and *Cloudcuckooland* (1996). He has also written four stage plays and two novels. He has received many awards for his writing, including the Forward Poetry Prize in 1992. In 1994 he was named *Sunday Times* Writer of the Year.

IT AIN'T WHAT YOU DO
IT'S WHAT IT DOES TO YOU

I have not bummed across America
with only a dollar to spare, one pair
of busted Levi's and a bowie knife.
I have lived with thieves in Manchester.

I have not padded through the Taj Mahal,   5
barefoot, listening to the space between
each footfall picking up and putting down
its print against the marble floor. But I

skimmed flat stones across Black Moss on a day
so still I could hear each set of ripples   10
as they crossed. I felt each stone's inertia
spend itself against the water; then sink.

I have not toyed with a parachute chord
while perched on the lip of a light aircraft;
but I held the wobbly head of a boy   15
at the day centre, and stroked his fat hands.

And I guess that the tightness in the throat
and the tiny cascading sensation
somewhere inside us are both part of that
sense of something else. That feeling, I mean.   20

GLOSSARY

3 *Levi's*: a brand of jeans

3 *bowie knife*: a strong, one-edged dagger knife

5 *Taj Mahal*: the most famous building in India, the magnificent mausoleum at Agra

9 *Black Moss*: a river on the border between Yorkshire and Lancashire.

11 *inertia*: stillness

18 *cascading*: falling (like a waterfall)

GUIDELINES

'It Ain't What You Do It's What It Does To You' is from the collection *Zoom!* (1989). The title of the poem echoes the song 'It ain't what you do it's the way that you do it'. Simon Armitage's work as a probation officer helps to explain some of his references in the poem.

The poem tells us about some of the adventurous things other people have done that the poet has not. For example, he hasn't travelled across America with little or no money, visited the Taj Mahal in India (one of the seven wonders of the world) or made a parachute jump from an aeroplane. Even though he has not been to India, he describes it in some detail, as if someone had told him about it. You can sense a certain regret, perhaps, that he has missed out on this particular experience, from the language he uses to convey its quietness and spirituality.

But he has his own experiences to relate. The things he has done may seem ordinary, such as living among thieves (we remember that he was a probation officer for a time), or skimming stones across a river. As in the description of the Taj Mahal, he makes use of the sounds of words to help us share in the experience of skimming stones. Notice the amount of 's' sounds he uses that create a musical effect, echoing the sound of water. It is as if this simple action was as significant to him as a visit to India would have been.

In the fourth stanza he mentions perhaps the most thrilling or dangerous thing he has not done – the parachute jump. But what he *has* done is communicate with, and comfort, another human being. The words suggest that this boy is special, perhaps unable to communicate by speech. It is a moving image that contrasts with the danger and excitement of the first two lines of the stanza.

In the last stanza the poet tries to express the effect that his own, more ordinary experiences have had on him. He uses his senses to get across the idea that these experiences have caused him to feel as emotional as more exciting adventures might have done. He suggests, too, that these feelings may also have a deeper, more spiritual significance, what he calls 'that / sense of something else'. The words are vague, as if he is attempting to describe the indescribable, and realises how difficult it is.

THE THEME OF THE POEM

The title of the poem gives us a good idea as to what its theme may be. What we actually do may not matter very much. What matters is how we respond to it and what effect it has on us as human beings. That is how we achieve fulfilment.

QUESTIONS

1 Why do you think the poet chooses the particular experiences that he has missed? What do they have in common with each other?

2 Do you think he regrets not having these experiences? Explain your answer.

3 Why did skimming the stones across the river and holding the boy's head at the day centre mean so much to him? What might these experiences have in common with each other, if anything?

4 What kind of feeling do you think Armitage is describing in the last stanza? Does he describe it well, in your opinion?

5 Which of the experiences described in the poem would you yourself like to share? Explain your answer.

6 From your reading of the poem, what sort of person do you imagine the speaker to be?

7 Does this poem make you think about life in a new way?

8 Do you think this poem appeals to young people in particular? Give reasons for your view.

EAVAN BOLAND

B. 1944

BIOGRAPHY

Eavan Boland was born in Dublin in 1944, the daughter of diplomat Frederick Boland and artist Frances Kelly. As a child she moved with her family from Dublin to live in London and later in New York, where her father had been appointed Ambassador to the United Nations. On her return to Ireland in her mid-teens, she completed her secondary school education at the Convent of the Holy Child, Killiney. Afterwards she studied English and Latin at Trinity College, Dublin.

In 1966 she was awarded a first-class degree in English. For a time she was a junior lecturer at Trinity College, but in 1967 she left the academic life, becoming a literary journalist with RTÉ and the *Irish Times* as well as concentrating on her career as a poet. In 1969 she married the novelist Kevin Casey and moved to the suburb of Dundrum at the foothill of the Dublin mountains. The couple have two daughters.

Eavan Boland's first book of poems, *New Territory,* was published in 1967. *The War Horse* followed in 1975. In 1979 she lived with her family for a year in Iowa, USA, where she lectured at the International Writing Program. Her next collection, *In Her Own Image* (1980), with its explicitly feminist themes, reflects her exposure to the North American women's movement. In 1980 she was also a co-founder of Arlen House, an Irish feminist press. *Night Feed* (1982) and *The*

Journey (1986) celebrate the reality of many women's lives, looking after children and tending the home.

The two collections *Outside History* (1990) and *In a Time of Violence* (1994) broadened the scope of these issues, exploring the place of women in the past. *Collected Poems* was published in 1995, followed by *The Lost Land* in 1998 and *Code* in 2001. She has written a number of stimulating prose essays about poetry and the role of the woman poet in society, in particular *Object Lessons* (1995). She is now Professor of English at Stanford University in California.

SOCIAL AND CULTURAL CONTEXT

In her poetic career, Eavan Boland has engaged with many interesting and controversial issues. As an undergraduate in Trinity College she was part of a gifted group of young poets that included Brendan Kennelly, Michael Longley and Derek Mahon. When she became a full-time poet, she was for a time involved in the Dublin literary scene, meeting poets such as Padraic Colum and Patrick Kavanagh. Later, when she had married and moved to the suburbs, she began to examine critically the Irish poetic tradition as represented by these male poets. Sensing that this tradition was primarily 'bardic and male', she has said: 'I couldn't find my life in poetry'. For her, she says, the kettle, the baby's bottle, the kitchen 'were parts of my world. Not to write about them would have been artificial.'

In the 1960 and 1970s, the influence of the feminist movement, arguably the most influential movement of the second half of the twentieth century, began to be felt in Ireland. Questions about the relationship of gender and power were being asked in the field of poetry as well as in the political sphere. Internationally, the example of poets like Sylvia Plath and Adrienne Rich offered scope to women to write about their experiences of marriage and motherhood. Eavan Boland has said that, for her, feminism has been an enabling perception. Her involvement with the feminist publishing house Arlen Press and creative writing workshops for women stemmed from her interest in women's issues. However, she has pointed out that though she is a feminist she is not a feminist poet: 'Poetry begins where the certainties end …Women writers have struggled to be heard … and it is very important that they are not part of silencing anyone else.'

In later years her interpretation of feminism broadened to include an examination of the position of women in the Irish poetic tradition. She has concluded that the complexity of real women's lives has been diminished by the association of femininity and Irishness in poetic emblems such as Caitlín Ní Houlihan and Dark Rosaleen. This, she contends, has ignored the lives lived by ordinary women in the past, by what she terms the 'lost, voiceless, the silent' women who were victims of the Irish famine or, like her own grandmother, who died in a fever hospital in Dublin in 1909.

Her engagement with these issues has strengthened her assertion that there has been, and will continue to be, change in the role of women in Irish literature. She has said that 'over a relatively short time – certainly no more than a generation or so – women have moved from being the subjects and objects of Irish poems to being the authors of them'. In this context, she became involved in the debate about the under-representation of women writers and editors in *The Field Day Anthology of Irish Literature* in 1992.

The nature of Irish identity and how it is portrayed in history and literature has been a subject of intellectual and political controversy in recent times, particularly since the onset of conflict in Northern Ireland in the 1970s. Eavan Boland has dealt with these issues in her work and in her public life. Her autobiographical collection of prose essays, *Object Lessons: the Life of the Woman and the Poet in Our Time,* gives valuable insights both into her development as a poet and into her perceptions of the challenges that she faces as a woman poet in our time.

CHILD OF OUR TIME

for Aengus

Yesterday I knew no lullaby
But you have taught me overnight to order
This song, which takes from your final cry
Its tune, from your unreasoned end its reason;
Its rhythm from the discord of your murder   5
Its motive from the fact you cannot listen.

We who should have known how to instruct
With rhymes for your waking, rhymes for your sleep,
Names for the animals you took to bed,
Tales to distract, legends to protect   10
Later an idiom for you to keep
And living, learn, must learn from you, dead,

To make our broken images rebuild
Themselves around your limbs, your broken
Image, find for your sake whose life our idle   15
Talk has cost, a new language. Child
Of our time, our times have robbed your cradle.
Sleep in a world your final sleep has woken.

GUIDELINES

'Child of Our time' is taken from *The War Horse* (1975). The precise date of the poem is 17 May, 1974, almost immediately after the bomb blasts that took place in Dublin in 1974.

Eavan Boland describes the genesis of the poem:

I wrote it inspired – and I use the word with care – by a photograph I saw two days later on the front of a national newspaper whose most arresting feature was the expression on the face of the fireman who lifted that child, an expression of tenderness as if he were lifting his own child from its cradle to its mother's breast.

She also writes of 'that greatest of obscenities, the murder of the innocent' and refers to her poem as 'one among many other statements of outrage'.

From the beginning, the two qualities of tenderness and outrage are evident in the tone of the poem. The formal elegy or lament, which the poem is, becomes in the first stanza a lullaby suitable for a child. But the musical imagery does not allow us to forget the utter horror of the child's death. Although the world of the child is lyrically evoked for us, there is a contrasting note of moral severity to be heard throughout. Adults should have known how to protect this child. Images of language, as of music, are significant: the 'idiom' of a society, the culture and values that it holds, should have been transmitted to this child. But now the roles are reversed, as the poem makes clear, and it is the adults who must learn from the child.

The image of language, of speech, takes on a further urgency in the final stanza. A new way of communication must be found if any progress can be made, if healing can take place. Maybe, paradoxically, the innocence of the child's death, his final sleep, might 'wake up' the world he once lived in.

Traditionally, an elegy had three main functions: to lament, to praise and to console. All three elements are to be found in 'Child of Our Time'. Rhyme and sound patterns add to the formality of the poem's intention. The poem also has a political dimension. The response is to a public tragedy that has occurred because of a breakdown in political relations. The undoubted anger in the poem is not directed at individuals, but at the irresponsibility of a society which has allowed such things to happen. What sort of 'times' do we live in, the poem implies, if an infant can be arbitrarily killed? How can we in Ireland find a new way of communicating with each other that does not include violence and murder? Although the poem is rooted in the conflict in Northern Ireland, the question nevertheless applies to the suffering and damage inflicted on children in all wars.

QUESTIONS

1 Would you agree that the poem expresses feelings both of tenderness and outrage? Where in the poem can we locate these contrasting feelings?

2 How is the world of childhood innocence evoked in the second stanza?

3 Trace the imagery of song, language and speech as used in the poem.

4 How does the sound of the poem contribute to its effect?

5 A political poem usually seeks to bring about change. Is 'Child of Our Time' an effective political poem, in your view?

6 As a poem, 'Child of Our time' communicates its theme by aesthetic means. Using the language of argument/persuasion, write out the speech you would make for or against the view that violence can never be justified.

THIS MOMENT

A neighbourhood.
At dusk.

Things are getting ready
to happen
out of sight.   5

Stars and moths.
And rinds slanting around fruit.

But not yet.

One tree is black.
One window is yellow as butter.   10

A woman leans down to catch a child
who has run into her arms
this moment.

Stars rise.
Moths flutter.   15
Apples sweeten in the dark.

GLOSSARY

7 *rinds slanting around fruit*: an unusual image, almost kinaesthetic in its sense of
movement. Even the rinds (peel) of the fruit appear to be 'getting ready' to
change as the moment will change

GUIDELINES

'This Moment' is from 'Legends', part two of the collection *In a Time of Violence*
(1994). The poem captures the essence of a particular moment in time in vivid,
sensuous images. The effect has the clarity of a painting.

The moment takes place at dusk, in itself a fleeting time of day. The setting
is a suburban neighbourhood. The focus is on what is actually happening at that

particular moment, but the intensity of the perception is heightened by an awareness, almost from the very beginning, that the moment will not last.

The only human figures in the poem are a woman and her child, running into her arms. The image reminds us, perhaps, in its timelessness, of the Madonna and Child. The language in the final stanza has rich connotations: 'sweeten' appeals both to our sense of smell and taste but it also has associations with the sweet smell of decay. If we remember too that an apple has Biblical associations (Adam and Eve ate from the Tree of Knowledge, traditionally an apple tree, and so lost Paradise for ever), we can see further associations with change and loss of innocence.

QUESTIONS

1 Would you agree that the poem is effective in evoking a particular moment? How does it do so?
2 Which of the adjectives best describe the atmosphere in this poem, in your opinion: peaceful, tender, strange? Perhaps you would suggest another word?
3 How does the poem make us aware of change?
4 Look at the form of the poem with its varying line lengths and stanza lengths. What effect do they contribute to the poem?
5 Eavan Boland has spoken of her desire to 'bless the ordinary, sanctify the common' in her poetry. To what extent does this short lyric succeed in this?
6 If you were to make a short film of this poem, what music/special effects would you use? What atmosphere would you try to create?

JOHN DONNE

1572–1631

BIOGRAPHY

Donne (pronounced 'done'), the son of a prosperous London merchant, was one of the most learned men in an age remarkable for learned men. His learning is constantly reflected in his poetry. He spent three years at Oxford and three at Cambridge. He was a student at the Inns of Court in London, where he studied law, languages and theology from four in the morning until ten.

Donne was born into an age of fierce, often deadly, religiously controversy. During the long reign of Elizabeth the First (1558–1603), Catholics were regarded as enemies of the state and many suffered torture, imprisonment and death for upholding their faith. Donne was brought up a Catholic. His mother was related by marriage to Sir Thomas More, the Lord Chancellor of England, who had been martyred in 1535 for refusing to acknowledge the claim of Henry VIII to be head of the English church. Four hundred years after his death, More was declared a saint by the Catholic Church. Donne's family suffered for their religion. His brother Henry died in 1593 after being arrested for concealing a priest. When he was about thirty, Donne abandoned his Catholic faith and became an Anglican. In 1615, he was ordained to the ministry of the Church of England.

As a young man, Donne was extremely ambitious, attaching himself to influential patrons as a means of advancing his career. He travelled in Europe and took part in two naval expeditions. He became secretary to Sir Thomas Egerton, a man of great power and influence. His hopes of worldly advancement were blighted when he secretly married Anne More, Egerton's niece, in 1601. She was seventeen, he almost thirty. Her father, who was Lieutenant of the Tower of London, used his power to ruin Donne's career, compelling Egerton to dismiss him and have him imprisoned. On his release, Donne had to take legal action to be reunited with his wife. He summarised the consequences of his imprudent marriage in a rueful, witty epigram ('John Donne – Anne Donne – Undone').

During his Anglican phase, Donne was a champion of his new religion, and wrote a good deal of anti-Catholic propaganda. His literary career has two broad divisions. His memorable secular poetry (love poems, elegies and satires) belongs to the first half of his life, when he enjoyed the society of women, and was especially fond of the theatre. Almost all his poetry, even the *Holy Sonnets*, was written before his ordination in 1615. This latter event marked a new phase in his literary career. He abandoned poetry for the composition of sermons, achieving fame as one of the outstanding preachers of his time. Fragments of these sermons, divorced from their original contexts, have long been part of popular discourse (for example, 'No man is an island' and 'never send to know for whom the bell tolls; it tolls for thee'). Donne's sermons are intensely personal, expressing remorse for past sins and, above all, his obsessive interest in his own death, which was the subject of his last sermon, preached before King Charles I. The point of the sermon was reinforced by what his first biographer called 'a decayed body and a dying face'. Death is also a major theme of his poetry.

Donne became Dean of St Paul's Cathedral in London in 1621. This promotion, as he himself put it, marked the rejection of 'the mistress of my youth, Poetry' for 'the wife of mine age, Divinity [Religion]'. The evidence suggests that Donne regarded himself as a writer of sermons rather than a poet. He published virtually nothing of his poetry and took no steps to collect or preserve it. On the other hand, he saw to it that his sermons were carefully preserved for publication. His literary contemporaries saw things differently. When his poems were published after his death, some of the principal writers of his time composed impressive tributes to his originality and his inventiveness. For over two centuries, his poetry was not highly regarded. In the eighteenth century, when elegance and grace were among the desirable features of poetry, Donne's verse was seen as awkward, primitive and inelegant, partly due to the fact that his work was available only in poor, inaccurate versions. The first good text of Donne's poems was that of Grierson (1912). Following the publication of T. S. Eliot's celebrated essay 'The Metaphysical Poets' in 1923, Donne came to be regarded as a major poet, admired above all for his unique blend of thought with feeling, his exciting use of argument and analogy, his mastery of a lively, colloquial idiom. Donne was now valued for his wit, expressed in what became known as the metaphysical conceit, which depended for its success on his ability to discover resemblances between apparently unrelated facts and ideas. There was also the delighted recognition of his constant readiness to surprise — his use of learned ideas in support of the most daring conclusions.

The Donne revival became a cult. Some important twentieth-century poets and critics, among them Eliot and Pound, were profoundly influenced by his poetry. The daring conceit with which Eliot opens 'The Love Song of J. Alfred Prufrock' is a famous example of this influence. Donne's poetry is necessarily élitist, given his tendency to exploit his massive, wide ranging store of knowledge. Donne appeals to the intelligence and knowledge of his readers, as well as to their imaginations. An appreciation of his poems depends ultimately on our ability to work at them in order to discover what their astonishingly broad range of reference meant to their author, and what it can mean almost four centuries later.

SOCIAL AND CULTURAL CONTEXT

Since Samuel Johnson's discussion of their work in his *Lives of the Poets* (1779–81), it has been customary to describe Donne, Herbert, Vaughan and Marvell (to mention only the greater figures) as the English Metaphysical poets. To give an account of some of the distinctive features of Donne's poetry is a convenient method of describing the outstanding characteristics of Metaphysical poetry.

One of the most remarkable things about Donne's poems is the extent to which they are taken up with arguments or attempts to persuade. Many of them are exercises in the use and abuse of logic. An astonishing example is 'The Flea', which consists of twenty-seven lines of witty, closely-knit argument on the significance for two lovers of a flea-bite. It is an argument designed to prove that if the speaker's mistress kills the flea, she will be committing murder, suicide and sacrilege. In his love poems, the speaker argues constantly with the woman he is addressing, trying to persuade her to share a point of view. In his religious poems, the 'Holy Sonnets' for example, he cannot refrain from arguing with God, to whom he addresses some outrageously witty and paradoxical appeals, such as in 'Batter my heart':

> *That I may rise and stand, o'erthrow me, and bend*
> *Your force, to break, blow, burn, and make me new.*

Much of Donne's poetry is dramatic, dealing vividly and directly with actual or imaginary experiences, situations and attitudes. His arresting, often startling openings are one aspect of his dramatic manner, illustrated for example in 'The Sunne Rising' ('Busie old foole, unruly Sunne'). Other dramatic features are the reader's sense of a situation, a speaker and someone being spoken to. As we read Donne's love poems and many of the sonnets, we have, more distinctly than in the case of almost any other poet, the impression of a living voice speaking from the page to us. The rhythms of Donne's verse are closer to those of living, colloquial speech than to those of most lyrical poems. Many of his poems are like performances by an actor enormously enjoying his brilliant displays of showmanship and virtuosity. The dramatic gifts displayed in the poems make it easy to understand why he was regarded as the greatest preacher of his age.

Donne is consistently witty, even in his very serious poems. Wit, arguably the essential feature of all Metaphysical poetry, implies quickness of intellect, the ability to say brilliant or sparkling things — to surprise or delight by means of unexpected thoughts or expressions. Donne's wit finds an outlet in outrageous arguments, paradoxes, puns and, above all, conceits. A paradox is a statement that on the surface seems self-contradictory but which turns out, on closer examination, to have a valid meaning that goes beyond the bounds of common sense and logic. The sonnet 'Batter my heart' is built around a series of powerful paradoxes. A conceit is a comparison, often extended, between things that at first sight seem to have little or nothing in common. A famous example is the comparison between lovers and compasses in 'A Valediction: forbidding mourning'. Those who do not like Donne's conceits tend to describe the comparisons they involve as far-fetched. Those who admire them stress the ingenuity, boldness and originality of the best examples.

Donne greatly extended the scope and subject-matter of poetic imagery. He takes his images from a very wide range of subjects. The furniture of his love poems is not limited to the assortment of stock properties traditionally employed by love poets, such as gardens, balconies, nightingales and so on. His speakers stimulate (or puzzle) the minds of loved ones with an impressively daunting array of images drawn from learned sources. Some of his most famous conceits are theological, medical or scientific, or are drawn from geographical discovery and exploration, the law or medieval philosophy. They are deployed in a witty, knowing, subtle way as, for example, in the opening line of his sonnet on death and final judgement, where the reference to 'the round earths imagin'd corners' is a clever indication that the speaker is familiar with both the old and the new astronomy. In Donne, learned images are balanced by others which are homely and realistic, drawn from the routines of daily life.

Donne introduced a new tone into English love poetry. The Elizabethan love poet tended to idealise the beloved, presenting her as a paragon of beauty and virtue to be thought and spoken of with reverence. Donne's love poetry can be impudent and insolent, sceptical and mocking, cynical and flippant. It is seldom idealistic, tender or reverential. His speakers think of the women they address as people who can respond to witty arguments and who might enjoy elaborate fooling or outrageous paradoxes. Dryden must have spoken for many puzzled readers when he declared that Donne 'perplexes the minds of the fair sex with nice speculations of philosophy when he should engage their hearts, and entertain them with the softness of love'. This comment may simply indicate that Donne had a higher opinion of the intellectual capacities of women than Dryden did. It may also mean that these two great poets held widely differing views on the nature of love poetry.

THE FLEA

Marke but this flea, and marke in this,
How little that which thou deny'st me is;
It suck'd me first, and now sucks thee,
And in this flea, our two bloods mingled bee;
Thou know'st that this cannot be said   5
A sinne, nor shame, nor losse of maidenhead,
    Yet this enjoyes before it wooe,
    And pamper'd swells with one blood made of two,
    And this, alas, is more than wee would doe.

Oh stay, three lives in one flea spare,   10
Where wee almost, yea more than maryed are.
This flea is you and I, and this
Our mariage bed, and mariage temple is;
Though parents grudge, and you, w'are met,
And cloysterd in these living walls of Jet,   15
    Though use make you apt to kill mee,
    Let not to that, selfe murder added bee,
    And sacrilege, three sinnes in killing three.

Cruell and sodaine, hast thou since
Purpled thy naile, in blood of innocence?   20
Wherein could this flea guilty bee,
Except in that drop which it suckt from thee?
Yet thou triumph'st, and saist that thou
Find'st not thy selfe, nor mee the weaker now;
    'Tis true, then learne how false, feares bee;   25
    Just so much honor, when thou yeeld'st to mee,
    Will wast, as this flea's death tooke life from thee.

  6 *maidenhead*: virginity

  9 *more … doe*: they don't want a pregnancy

  stay … spare: refrain from killing the flea, and so spare three lives all at once (the flea's, yours and mine). Since their 'two bloods' are mingled in the flea because it bit both of them, he imagines both their lives present in its body

  11 *maryed*: married

  15 *cloysterd … Jet*: lodged inside the walls of the flea's black body

  16 *use*: habit

17–18 *Let not … three*: don't add suicide and sacrilege to murder. She will be guilty of sacrilege if, by killing the flea, she destroys the temple in which they were married

  19 *sodaine*: sudden, impulsive

  since: already

  20 *Purpled thy naile*: she has crushed the flea to death with her nails

  21 *Wherein*: in what way

25–7 *then learne … thee*: she will lose no more of her honour by yielding to him than the flea took from her when he sucked her blood.

GUIDELINES

Flea poems were very common in European Renaissance literature. They were generally indecent. Here Donne deflects attention from the woman's body and focuses instead on the body of the flea. By sucking the speaker's blood and then that of his mistress, the flea becomes a symbol of the union he desires with her. Donne displays extraordinary ingenuity and skill in his witty exploration in the implications of a fleabite.

QUESTIONS

1 Here the flea appears in a variety of guises. List these. How appropriate are they to Donne's theme?
2 What is Donne trying to achieve in the poem?
3 Discuss 'The Flea' as an example of Donne's astonishing ingenuity and verbal dexterity.
4 Is the flea the central character of this poem?
5 Outline the argument of the poem in your own words.
6 On the evidence of the poem, what kind of woman is Donne addressing?

SONG: GOE AND CATCHE A FALLING STARRE

Goe, and catche a falling starre,
    Get with child a mandrake roote,
Tell me, where all past yeares are,
    Or who cleft the Divels foot,
Teach me to heare Mermaides singing,   5
    Or to keep off envies stinging,
        And finde
        What winde
Serves to advance an honest minde.

If thou beest borne to strange sights   10
    Things invisible to see,
Ride ten thousand daies and nights,
    Till age snow white haires on thee,
Thou, when thou retorn'st, wilt tell mee
All strange wonders that befell thee,   15
        And sweare
        No where
Lives a woman true, and faire.

If thou findst one, let mee know,
    Such a Pilgrimage were sweet;   20
Yet doe not, I would not goe,
    Though at next doore wee might meet,
Though shee were true, when you met her,
And last, till you write your letter,
        Yet shee   25
        Will bee
False, ere I come, to two, or three.

Goe … minde: the speaker lists a number of impossible tasks

  2 *Get … root*: make a mandrake root pregnant. The mandrake, a plant with forked roots, was believed to have human qualities

  4 *Who cleft the Divels foot*: the devil was said to have a cloven hoof

12 *Ride … nights*: this recalls the story of a squire who engaged in a three-year countrywide search for a chaste woman, and eventually found one: a plain countrywoman, whom he could not corrupt

18 *Lives a woman true, and faire*: the most unlikely of all discoveries would be a woman who was faithful as well as beautiful

20 *were*: would be

21 *doe not*: do not tell me

23–7 *Though … or three*: the pilgrim might find a beautiful woman who was faithful when he met her. However, by the time the speaker reached her in response to this news, she would have been unfaithful to two or three men.

GUIDELINES

The theme of this witty, extravagant poem is the infidelity of women, particularly beautiful women. It is, the argument of the poem goes, as hard to find a beautiful woman who is at the same time faithful and chaste as it is to perform traditionally impossible tasks.

QUESTIONS

1 Does the speaker really believe the argument he is advancing in this poem?
2 What is the mood of the poem: is the speaker being cynical, sad, pessimistic, lighthearted or satirical for example? Or can he be serious?
3 What does the poem tell you about the kind of person the speaker is?
4 What is the significance of the reference to 'a Pilgrimage' in line 20?
5 Contrast the ideas and attitudes of this poem with those of 'The Flea'.

CAROL ANN DUFFY

B. 1955

BIOGRAPHY

Carol Ann Duffy was born in Glasgow in December 1955. She grew up in Staffordshire where she was educated at Stafford Girls' High School. She studied philosophy at university in Liverpool before moving to London to work as a freelance writer. She has written plays as well as poems, edited books of poetry and been a writer-in-residence at the Southern Arts, Thamesdown. She has lived in Manchester where she lectured in poetry at Manchester Metropolitan University.

Duffy has published several volumes of poems, among them *Standing Female Nude* (1985), *Selling Manhattan* (1987), *The Other Country* (1990) and *Mean Time* (1993). In 2000 she published *The World's Wife*, a collection of dramatic monologues in the voices of the wives of famous men (Mrs Midas and Mrs Aesop, for example). She has edited two anthologies for teenagers, *I Wouldn't Thank You for a Valentine* and *Stopping for Death*.

Carol Ann Duffy has been awarded many prizes for her work, among them the Forward Poetry Prize and the Whitbread Poetry Award. In 1995 she was awarded an OBE in the Queen's Birthday Honours List. She is one of the most popular women poets writing today.

VALENTINE

Not a red rose or a satin heart.

I give you an onion.
It is a moon wrapped in brown paper.
It promises light
like the careful undressing of love.   5

Here.
It will blind you with tears
like a lover.
It will make your reflection
a wobbling photo of grief.   10

I am trying to be truthful.

Not a cute card or a kissogram.

I give you an onion.
Its fierce kiss will stay on your lips,
possessive and faithful   15
as we are,
for as long as we are.

Take it.
Its platinum loops shrink to a wedding-ring,
if you like.   20

Lethal.
Its scent will cling to your fingers,
cling to your knife.

GLOSSARY

19 *platinum*: white, valuable metal used in jewellery

21 *Lethal*: deadly, dangerous

GUIDELINES

'Valentine' is from the collection *Mean Time* (1993). Like a traditional valentine, the poem contains a proposal of marriage. But unlike a traditional valentine, the proposal is expressed in unromantic terms.

The title prepares us for a romantic love poem, but what we find is rather different. Instead of the usual sorts of gifts like red roses and satin hearts, the lover gives her beloved an onion.

The speaker makes a case for the onion as an appropriate gift. The metaphors are unusual, in that ordinary things (brown paper) are mixed with romantic images (the moon). This mixture of ordinary and romantic continues through the poem and gives it its ironic, bittersweet tone, so that we are never quite sure what exactly the feelings of the speaker are. For instance, the speaker never allows us to forget that the gift is an onion, so that we find references to its layers of skin, its colour, the fact that peeling onions makes us cry, and yet each of these aspects is made to fit the speaker's view of love: that it is sexual, that it offers light and happiness, but that it can also make you cry.

The speaker thinks that an onion is a more 'truthful' symbol of love than any other more conventional Valentine's Day gift. She reveals even more clearly what she thinks love is. The smell and taste of the onion, its 'fierce kiss', will last on the lips of the beloved, just as the speaker's love will last – as long as the love they share will last. Here she seems to recognise that love may not last forever, another more honest view of love than is usually found in a valentine.

There is a sense that the speaker is appealing to her beloved – 'Take it' – as she reveals another aspect of the onion that makes it appropriate. Its white rings, as it is cut up, may become 'platinum hoops' like a wedding ring, as the speaker says rather uncertainly 'if you like'. It is as if she is not totally confident about the relationship, so that the proposal comes across as rather off-hand and casual.

You can read the final three lines in a number of ways. 'Lethal' might suggest the fierceness of love, but it has underlying suggestions of destruction. And is there a threatening tone in the image of the onion's scent that 'clings'? 'Knife' is a strange word to finish with in a poem about love. Does it have suggestions of bitterness and betrayal?

How we respond to the poem may depend on our own personal experience, but we cannot fail to see how original and honest it is.

QUESTIONS

1 Why, according to the poem's speaker, is the onion suitable as a gift for the beloved on Valentine's Day?

2 Which of the metaphors and similes that the poet uses do you find the most unusual and effective?

3 Do you think the relationship between the lovers in this poem is a happy one?

4 What attitude to love and relationships in general is suggested in this poem?

5 Do you find the speaker's vision of love honest, bitter, refreshing, off-putting? Perhaps you would prefer to use another word?

6 Imagine you are the person who has received the onion (and the poem) as a valentine. Write out the response you would make.

PAUL
DURCAN

B. 1944

BIOGRAPHY

Paul Durcan was born in Dublin in October 1944. He studied first at UCD, but left without taking a degree. Later, he graduated with a BA in Archaeology and Medieval History from University College, Cork.

Durcan has published many collections of poetry, among them *The Berlin Wall Café* (1985), *Daddy, Daddy* (1990), *Crazy about Women* (1991), *Greetings to our Friends in Brazil* (1999) and *Cries of an Irish Caveman* (2001). *Daddy Daddy* won the prestigious Whitbread Prize for Poetry.

Paul Durcan has given readings of his poetry throughout Ireland and Britain and in many other parts of the world, including Russia and Brazil. His poetry readings are dramatic, entertaining occasions. He regularly broadcasts on RTÉ, reading his own work and speaking about literature.

Paul Durcan has lived in London and Barcelona as well as Dublin, where he now resides. He is one of Ireland's most well-known poets.

GOING HOME TO MAYO, WINTER, 1949

Leaving behind us the alien, foreign city of Dublin
My father drove through the night in an old Ford Anglia,
His five-year-old son in the seat beside him,
The rexine seat of red leatherette,
And a yellow moon peered in through the windscreen.   5
'Daddy, Daddy,' I cried, 'Pass out the moon,'
But no matter how hard he drove he could not pass out the moon.
Each town we passed through was another milestone
And their names were magic passwords into eternity:
Kilcock, Kinnegad, Strokestown, Elphin,   10
Tarmonbarry, Tulsk, Ballaghaderreen, Ballavarry;
Now we were in Mayo and the next stop was Turlough,
The village of Turlough in the heartland of Mayo,
And my father's mother's house, all oil-lamps and women,
And my bedroom over the public bar below,   15
And in the morning cattle-cries and cock-crows:
Life's seemingly seamless garment gorgeously rent
By their screeches and bellowings. And in the evenings
I walked with my father in the high grass down by the river
Talking with him – an unheard-of thing in the city.   20

But home was not home and the moon could be no more outflanked
Than the daylight nightmare of Dublin city:
Back down along the canal we chugged into the city
And each lock-gate tolled our mutual doom;
And railings and palings and asphalt and traffic-lights,   25
And blocks after blocks of so-called 'new' tenements –
Thousands of crosses of loneliness planted
In the narrowing grave of the life of the father;
In the wide, wide cemetery of the boy's childhood.

GLOSSARY

2 *Ford Anglia*: a brand of car

4 *rexine*: artificial leather used in upholstery

10 *Kilcock …Elphin*: Kilcock is in Co. Kildare; Kinnegad is in Co. Westmeath; Strokestown and Elphin are in Co. Roscommon

11 *Tarmonbarry, Tulsk, Ballaghaderreen, Ballavarry*: Co. Roscommon

12 *Turlough*: village in Co. Mayo, the birthplace of Paul Durcan's father

17 *rent*: torn

21 *outflanked*: passed out

24 *lock-gate*: gate for opening or closing a lock in a canal

25 *palings*: fences

25 *asphalt*: paving

26 *tenements*: houses divided into flats

GUIDELINES

Paul Durcan's parents came from Co. Mayo, where he spent many happy summer holidays as a child. In this poem he looks back to his childhood experience of travelling to Mayo with his father and his feelings about being there and returning to Dublin. Durcan's father was a circuit court judge, with whom the poet later had a rather troubled relationship.

From the beginning the speaker seems to see Dublin as an 'alien, foreign' place, possibly echoing his father's view of it (as a Mayoman). He describes the excitement of travelling in the car as a child, the childish desire to 'Pass out the moon', the sense of 'magic' as he names the towns through which they passed.

Vivid images of what he saw and heard bring to life his experience of actually being in Mayo on his holidays. Repetition of 'and' echoes his childish excitement. But there is a certain sadness in the image that ends the first stanza: he and his father, talking together, relax in a way that would not have happened in Dublin.

The atmosphere of the second stanza contrasts utterly with the first. Whereas life in Mayo was magical, life in Dublin was a 'daylight nightmare'. As the poet and his father return home through the city we can almost feel the weight of depression descending on him. Now the images suggest a sense of being trapped ('railings', 'palings'), the blocks of new tenements or Corporation flats becoming a metaphor for a kind of death and burial, for both himself and his father. The word 'loneliness' suggests that their return marked the end of the closeness that they had in Mayo.

QUESTIONS

1 What impression do you get of the relationship between the poet and his father as they travel to Mayo?

2 Do you think the use of placenames adds to the effect of the poem? Give reasons.

3 Contrast the poet's attitude to Mayo with his attitude to Dublin. Look carefully at the poet's use of language.

4 Do you think Durcan describes his childhood experience well? Give reasons for your view.

5 How would you describe the tone of the poem? Angry? Disappointed? Nostalgic? Sad? Perhaps you would suggest another word?

6 Do you like this poem? Give reasons for your answer.

7 You want to make a short film of this poem. Describe the sort of atmosphere you would like to create, and say what music, sound effects and images you would use.

ROBERT FROST

1874–1963

BIOGRAPHY

Robert Frost was born in San Francisco in 1874. At the age of eleven, following the death of his father, Frost moved with his family to New England. He attended Dartmouth College but failed to finish his undergraduate course, taking a job at a mill instead. He started to study again in 1897 at Harvard University, but left without taking a degree. He tried shoemaking, teaching, editing a local paper and then farming. In 1895 he married Elinor White, to whom he was married for forty-three years. They had six children, one of whom died in infancy. For a number of years the family lived on a farm which Frost had inherited from his grandfather. He also supplemented his income by teaching, which he enjoyed. However in 1911 Frost sold the farm and moved to England, where he hoped to find literary success.

His first book of poems, *A Boy's Will*, was published in England in 1913. His originality was recognised by leading poet and fellow American Ezra Pound, who praised Frost for having 'the good sense to speak naturally and to paint the thing, the thing as he sees it'. W. B. Yeats, too, called the volume 'the best poetry written in America for a long time'.

Frost now began to enjoy the friendship and acceptance of the English literary society of the time. His second collection, *North of Boston* (1914), received excellent reviews.

Having returned to America in 1915, Frost and his family settled on a farm in New Hampshire. The life of a farmer appealed to him. His experience of rural life is reflected in his third collection, *Mountain Interval* (1916), in which several of his most famous lyrics appear.

His life now combined farming, family life, writing and lecturing. This was very much the pattern that would continue for the rest of his life. He was a gifted speaker, with his mixture of homespun Yankee wisdom, poetic insights and sense of humour. Invitations to speak and read his poems around the country poured in. The collection *New Hampshire* (1923) consolidated his already formidable reputation, and in 1924 he was awarded the first of four Pulitzer Prizes for Poetry which he won during his lifetime, a record number for any poet. *West-Running Brook* (1928) was followed by the *Collected Poems* in 1931. In the same year he was elected to the American Academy of Arts and Letters. Many honorary degrees and public awards followed. His other published collections were *A Further Range* (1936), *A Witness Tree* (1942), *Steeple Bush* (1947) and his last collection, *In the Clearing* (1962).

Frost's public success was not mirrored by his personal life. He himself suffered from depression. One of his daughters died at the age of twenty-nine. His wife Elinor died in 1938. His only son committed suicide in 1940. Although Frost does not refer directly to these events, it may be that the trauma of these experiences is reflected in the occasional darkness of his poems.

Robert Frost died in 1963 at the age of 89.

SOCIAL AND CULTURAL CONTEXT

Although he was a contemporary of many of the great Modernist poets of the twentieth century, such as T. S. Eliot, Ezra Pound and Wallace Stevens, Robert Frost's work differs from theirs in certain important respects. Poets of the Modernist movement were influenced by the great developments in human thought in philosophy and science that had taken place at the end of the nineteenth century, notably the work of Sigmund Freud in psychoanalysis and Charles Darwin in science. The experience of the First World War, too, altered social attitudes and structures. It no longer seemed artistically credible to write poems in the traditional metres and forms. Indeed, the central tenet of the Modernist movement, articulated by Ezra Pound, was 'make it new'.

For a time Frost was part of the literary circle in London which included Ezra Pound. However, his poetic practice was not unduly influenced by ideas current at the time. His own career took a different path. Much of the work of Modernist poets was so experimental that it could be obscure, resulting in small sales for their books. Frost, on the other hand, set out to be understood.

From the beginning, he was a traditionalist in form and metre. He avoided writing in free verse. The settings of his poems are for the most part rural, whereas the Modernists saw themselves as the poets of the metropolis. Their works allude constantly to classical literature, while Frost's poems were praised for their accessibility. He was nonetheless a learned man who wished to develop his art in an independent and ambitious way. Early in his career he had a self-confident sense of purpose. As he wrote to a friend, John Bartlett: 'To be perfectly frank with you I am one of the most notable craftsmen of my time. That will transpire presently.'

He developed a sophisticated theory of poetic language which he called the 'sound of sense'. By this he meant that language in poetry should reproduce the exact tone of meaning in human speech. He recognised that his theory was not altogether original as the Romantic poets had put forward the idea that literary language should be as close as possible to 'the language of men' as far back as the late eighteenth century. But by the end of the nineteenth century, the diction of poetry had ceased to have common currency, and Frost, like Modernist poets also, searched for a new idiom in which to write.

The story of Frost's subsequent career as a poet is interesting in the light it throws upon cultural attitudes in America. His success can be partly explained by the way he deliberately built up a public persona of himself as a typical Yankee – a plain man living in rural New England, a man for whom the hard work of farming was a real inspiration. Biographers and critics have discussed the extent to which this persona was real or invented. They point out that he was a distinguished teacher and intellectual. Nor are his poems the simple 'nature' poems that they seem to be on the surface. As he said himself: 'I'm not a nature poet. There's always something else in my poetry.' But he continued to play a role that appealed to the public as an essentially American poet rooted in rural values. The Caribbean poet, Derek Walcott describes him: 'Robert Frost: the icon of Yankee values, the smell of wood-smoke, the sparkle of dew, the reality of farm-house dung, the jocular honesty of an uncle'.

Social historians point out that in the twentieth century, the American way of life became increasingly urbanised and remote from the rustic idylls Frost's poems seem to depict. It may be that nostalgia played a part in the public acclaim of Robert Frost. Certainly in social and cultural terms he had a prominent role in American public life. During the Second World War, 50,000 copies of one of his poems were distributed to US troops stationed overseas to boost morale. Honours and awards were heaped upon him during the course of his long life. His standing in American society can be seen clearly by his participation in president John F. Kennedy's Inauguration in 1961, while in 1962 he was asked to visit Russia on a goodwill mission for the US Department of State.

His place in the canon of American literature is assured both as a poet who influenced the course of the lyric poem as written by American poets, and as a best-selling poet whose work is part of the cultural birthright of the American people.

"OUT, OUT—"

The buzz saw snarled and rattled in the yard
And made dust and dropped stove-length sticks of wood,
Sweet-scented stuff when the breeze drew across it.
And from there those that lifted eyes could count
Five mountain ranges one behind the other   5
Under the sunset far into Vermont.
And the saw snarled and rattled, snarled and rattled,
As it ran light, or had to bear a load.
And nothing happened: day was all but done.
Call it a day, I wish they might have said   10
To please the boy by giving him the half hour
That a boy counts so much when saved from work.
His sister stood beside them in her apron
To tell them "Supper." At the word, the saw,
As if to prove saws knew what supper meant,   15
Leaped out of the boy's hand, or seemed to leap—
He must have given the hand. However it was,
Neither refused the meeting. But the hand!
The boy's first outcry was a rueful laugh,
As he swung toward them holding up the hand,   20
Half in appeal, but half as if to keep
The life from spilling. Then the boy saw all—
Since he was old enough to know, big boy
Doing a man's work, though a child at heart—
He saw all spoiled. "Don't let him cut my hand off—   25
The doctor, when he comes. Don't let him, sister!"
So. But the hand was gone already.
The doctor put him in the dark of ether.
He lay and puffed his lips out with his breath.
And then—the watcher at his pulse took fright.   30
No one believed. They listened at his heart.
Little—less—nothing!—and that ended it.
No more to build on there. And they, since they
Were not the one dead, turned to their affairs.

GUIDELINES

'Out, Out—' is from the collection *Mountain Interval* (1916). One of Robert Frost's most affecting poems, it is based on a true story. In 1910 the child of one of Frost's neighbours in Vermont, New England, died as a result of an accident on his father's farm. The local newspaper, *The Littleton Courier*, reported the incident like this:

> *Raymond Tracy Fitzgerald, one of the twin sons of Michael G. and Margaret Fitzgerald of Bethlehem, died at his home Thursday afternoon, March 24, as a result of an accident by which one of his hands was badly hurt in a sawing machine. The young man was assisting in sawing up some wood in his own dooryard with a sawing machine and accidentally hit the loose pulley, causing the saw to descend upon his hand, cutting and lacerating it very badly. Raymond was taken into the house and a physician was immediately summoned, but he died very suddenly from the effects of shock, which produced heart failure.*

Frost's narrative poem dramatises the incident reported above. The scene is set in the yard of the New England farm. From the beginning, the saw seems to be almost like another character in the drama, personified by 'snarled', with ominous implications. Without direct comment, the poem conveys a great deal about the hardworking and possibly even harsh conditions in which the boy lives and ultimately dies, adding to the sense of impending doom as the poem proceeds.

Critics have paid attention to the strangeness of the image of the saw as an animate object seemingly looking on the boy's hand as its 'supper'. And the line that follows almost goes so far as to suggest that the boy willed his death, or at least did nothing to prevent it.

But it is the depiction of the boy's death itself that has attracted most comment. The boy knows he is facing death: 'He saw all spoiled'. The word 'spoiled' suggests simply that the boy's future is spoiled, as of course it is. Frost's biographer Jay Parini interprets 'spoiled' as referring to the family dynamic that is now altered for ever:

The boy has subliminally come to understand that within the framework of a subsistence economy there is small room for a boy who cannot pull his weight. Circumstances are such that an extra 'hand' is essential for survival.

Such a reading, although harsh, fits in with the tone of the concluding lines of the poem.

The boy's death is described with no expression of grief or consolatory comment. But it is the reaction of those who are still living that takes us aback: 'And they, since they / Were not the one dead, turned to their affairs'.

QUESTIONS

1 Would you agree that there is a sense of foreboding in the poem from the beginning? How is this sense created?

2 What impression of rural life is given in the poem? How did you respond to it?

3 Are there any particular lines in the poem that puzzle or disturb you? Can you say why?

4 What might the poet be suggesting in the line beginning 'Then the boy saw all …'?

5 Examine the last two lines of the poem. Do you think this is an appropriate way to respond to a tragic death such as this? Do you find the effect chilling, callous, resigned, accepting, realistic? Perhaps your response could be described in an entirely different way? You might link your response with the impression of rural life you get from reading the entire poem.

6 Would you agree that this is a dramatic poem? Take into account the setting, characters, climax and ending, as well as the poem's title.

7 Do you like this poem?

THE ROAD NOT TAKEN

Two roads diverged in a yellow wood,
And sorry I could not travel both
And be one traveler, long I stood
And looked down one as far as I could
To where it bent in the undergrowth;   5

Then took the other, as just as fair,
And having perhaps the better claim,
Because it was grassy and wanted wear;
Though as for that, the passing there
Had worn them really about the same,   10

And both that morning equally lay
In leaves no step had trodden black.
Oh, I kept the first for another day!
Yet knowing how way leads on to way,
I doubted if I should ever come back.   15

I shall be telling this with a sigh
Somewhere ages and ages hence:
Two roads diverged in a wood, and I—
I took the one less traveled by,
And that has made all the difference.   20

GUIDELINES

'The Road Not Taken' is from *Mountain Interval* (1916). It is said to have been inspired by Frost's friend, the poet Edward Thomas, whom he had met in England and who was subsequently killed in the First World War. Thomas was apparently in the habit of expressing regret at whatever decision he had taken.

The poem dramatises the choices we are presented with in life and their consequences. The poet uses the metaphor of two roads, one of which he had to take. He then reflects on the choice he made. Not only does he review the reasons for his decision, such as they were, but he visualises himself examining it at some time in the future.

The poem is one of Robert Frost's most popular and often-quoted poems, no doubt because it deals with a universal theme. A number of interpretations have been put forward. Is the poem concerned with choice of career in life? (We may remember that Robert Frost himself left his life as a farmer in New England to develop his gifts as a poet.) Or does the poem hint at a moral struggle that has to be confronted, in which the least popular and most difficult option is chosen? And how do we interpret the last lines of the poem?

The setting of the poem is extremely attractive, with the 'yellow wood' evoking the famous New England fall. As in many of Frost's poems, images of nature are described not merely for their own sake, but to suggest an analogy with human concerns.

QUESTIONS

1 How are the 'two roads' presented, as they appeared to the speaker?
2 Can you trace the speaker's train of thought as he makes his decision?
3 Do you think the speaker is happy with his decision? How can we tell from the tone of the poem? Look especially at the last stanza.
4 Can you speculate about the choices in Frost's life (or anyone else's) that may be symbolised in this poem?
5 What do you think the poet means by the final line: 'And that has made all the difference'?
6 Can you understand why this is a well-loved poem in America and elsewhere?

ACQUAINTED WITH THE NIGHT

I have been one acquainted with the night.
I have walked out in rain—and back in rain.
I have outwalked the furthest city light.

I have looked down the saddest city lane.
I have passed by the watchman on his beat   5
And dropped my eyes, unwilling to explain.

I have stood still and stopped the sound of feet
When far away an interrupted cry
Came over houses from another street,

But not to call me back or say good-by;   10
And further still at an unearthly height
One luminary clock against the sky

Proclaimed the time was neither wrong nor right.
I have been one acquainted with the night.

GLOSSARY

12 *luminary clock*: a clock that gives out light (possibly the moon)

GUIDELINES

This short lyric, a sonnet, is from *West-Running Brook* (1928). The poem is unusual among Frost's work in that it is set in the city rather than in rural surroundings. It depicts the dark, alienating side of urban existence. The speaker in the poem experiences a sense of deep depression and loneliness as he walks through the city streets.

The title of the poem and the first line set up a rich association of ideas for the reader. It seems clear that the 'night' is not meant purely literally but also reflects the 'dark night of the soul' that the speaker has experienced. Nature itself seems to echo his sadness and despair. There is a suggestion of hidden violence in the city. But what strikes the reader most perhaps is the sense of isolation that the poem expresses. It may be that the 'luminary clock' he sees (possibly the moon or an actual lit-up clock) symbolises, in a general way, the passage of time. Its message, 'the time was neither wrong nor right', is slightly mysterious. Is it saying that time is indifferent to those who live in the isolation of the city? That right or wrong is irrelevant in urban life? It may also echo Hamlet's expression of despair in Shakespeare's play: 'The time is out of joint'.

The poem is a sonnet of fourteen lines, but it is not divided into the traditional octave and sestet or three quatrains and a couplet. Instead there are four tercets (three-line stanzas) and a couplet with the rhyming pattern *aba bcb cdc ded aa*. Apart from the rhyming couplet, this rhyme pattern corresponds to what is called *terza rima*. The Italian poet Dante, who invented the form, wrote in his *Inferno* about a descent into hell. Frost would have had this in mind as he chose the form in which to express his own sense of despair.

Critics have pointed out that 'Acquainted with the Night' shows Robert Frost's awareness of the themes and poetic technique of modernist poets of the early twentieth century, such as T. S. Eliot and Ezra Pound, for whom the city was an image of alienation. It may be that in this poem Robert Frost reveals some of his darkest fears about living – fears that were reflected in his frequent bouts of depression and psychosomatic illness during his lifetime. One of Frost's critics, Lionel Trilling, caused quite a stir when he once referred to Frost as 'a tragic poet whose work conceived of a terrifying universe'. Poems such as 'Acquainted with the Night', would bear out this perception of Frost's vision.

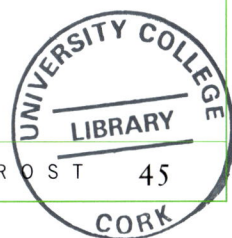

QUESTIONS

1 What do you think the poet suggests when he says that he has been 'acquainted with the night'? How do the images that follow develop this opening statement?

2 Would you agree that the sound of the poem echoes the poet's emotions? Look, for instance, at the rhymes used, the rhythm within the lines, the repetitions and the onomatopoeic effects of the long vowel sounds.

3 How is the indifference of the city suggested in the imagery of the poem?

4 What insight does the poem give us into Robert Frost as a person, in your opinion?

5 Do you find this poem different in tone from other poems by Frost on your course?

6 How did you respond to the theme and mood of the poem?

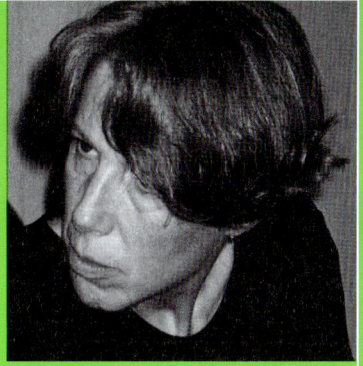

KERRY HARDIE

B. 1951

BIOGRAPHY

Kerry Hardie was born in 1951 in Singapore, Malaysia, but grew up in County Down. She studied English at York University, England and then came back to work as a researcher and radio interviewer for the BBC in Belfast and Derry. She writes:

> This period coincided with the most violent years of the Troubles, and through my job I had access to situations and people I might not otherwise have known. I became fascinated with people who found themselves in a hard place and with how they reacted to this place. Some people adapted astonishingly fast to their new realities, but others spent their energies resisting and could only change to meet them when they had in some way been broken by them.

Because of her background and because she now lives in Kilkenny, she says her writing is 'one way of joining up the island, of subverting the separateness that eighty years of government under different systems has reinforced'.

She has published three collections of poetry: *A Furious Place* (1996), *Cry for the Hot Belly* (2000) and *The Sky Didn't Fall* (2003). Her first novel, *A Winter Marriage*, was published by in 2002, and her second novel, *The Bird Woman*, in 2005.

Kerry Hardie has won major literary awards, including the Friends Provident National Poetry Prize, the 1995 Hennessey Award for Poetry, the 1996 UK National Poetry Prize and a 2004 James Joyce Foundation Award (which took her to China and Australia). She has also collected awards from American universities.

Kerry Hardie's first collection, *A Furious Place*, from which 'May' is taken, includes poems that record people in their own landscapes and explore the way in which landscape permeates their lives. In her novel, *A Winter Marriage*, the landscape and climate of an Irish winter is unbearable to the foreign woman who marries a local farmer. Other poems in *A Furious Place* dwell on the hardships and lessons of a chronic illness. Kerry Hardie suffers from ME (chronic fatigue syndrome):

> *Being chronically sick makes you an observer rather than a participant. Before I was sick, I lived very hard and my life was very outgoing; now my life is quiet and disciplined and reflective .. .It took me a long time to come to terms with the change, but now I find my life immensely rich and rewarding.*

Kerry Hardie lives in Kilkenny with her husband, Sean, who is also a writer.

MAY

For Marian

The blessèd stretch and ease of it –
heart's ease. The hills blue. All the flowering weeds
bursting open. Balm in the air. The birdsong
bouncing back out of the sky. The cattle
lain down in the meadows, forgetting to feed.   5
The horses swishing their tails.
The yellow flare of furze on the near hill.
And the first cream splatters of blossom
High on the thorns where the day rests longest.

All hardship, hunger, treachery of winter forgotten.   10
The unfounded conviction: forgiveness, hope.

GLOSSARY

3 *Balm*: a healing and soothing fragrance

7 *furze*: gorse, a prickly shrub with an abundance of yellow flowers which grows wild on hills and mountains

10 *treachery*: deceit or betrayal

11 *unfounded conviction*: a strong belief that has no foundation

GUIDELINES

'May' is an intriguing poem. Who speaks the words – the poet, or a persona, like a character in a novel? Is it a man or a woman? A stranger or a native? Someone who is content or someone who is unhappy? Does the speaker speak for all of us? Experiment with different readings of the poem until you find the voice which you think works best.

At first glance this is a simple poem about the effect of the weather and the seasons on our moods and emotions. It is a hymn of celebration to the long days of May and the sense of well-being they bring after winter. However, there are elements in the poem which may hint at a darker, more complicated meaning, although this is not necessarily a better reading of the poem than a more straight-forward one.

The speaker of the poem treats the long, easeful days of May as something blessed, as days which provide ease for the heart. The phrase, 'hearts' ease', may suggest that the speaker's heart is not easy and May brings respite from a life that is troubled. The word 'Balm' may also suggest that the speaker is in need of soothing or healing. The images of May evoke colour ('blue', 'yellow' and 'cream') and also the countryside ('weeds', 'furze' and 'thorns') bursting into flower. The energy of May is caught in the colourful verbs and the alliteration and onomatopoeia of the descriptive language. There is birdsong and the cattle and the horses take their ease in the fine weather. The cattle are so content that they forget 'to feed', something that would not happen in the hungry months of winter. The word 'rests' in line 9, taken alongside 'ease' (line 1), 'heart's ease' (line 2) and 'Balm' (line 3), seem to suggest a life that is in need of restoration or recuperation.

The two lines that conclude the poem put the previous nine lines in context. May is blessed because it finally puts paid to the hardship, hunger and treachery of winter, and although these are forgotten, they cast a long shadow over the poem. 'Hardship' and 'hunger' describe the physical harshness of winter but they may also refer to the life of the heart and the spirit. In similar fashion the word 'treachery' describes the treacherous weather of winter but it may also refer to a human treachery. What is clear is that the speaker states that May brings the 'unfounded conviction' of 'forgiveness and hope'. The last line will repay careful thought. Are the hope and forgiveness of the final line real or merely longed-for? Are they understandable? Do we all feel them in May? What does the final line tell us about someone (all of us?) who cling to unfounded convictions? What does it tell us about the human heart?

QUESTIONS

1 Then first nine lines are a feast of sensuous responses to the month of May. Comment on each image and the sense it celebrates.

2 The images include references to 'weeds' (line 2), 'furze' (line 7) and 'thorns' (line 9). Why, do you think, were these plants chosen?

3 How is the energy of May reflected in the language of the first nine lines?

4 Select one phrase and comment on the way it sounds and the poetic techniques Kerry Hardie uses to achieve this sound.

5 Why does the poet associate May with 'heart's ease'?

6 In what way is line 10 surprising?

7 What word strikes you with most force in line 10?

8 Imagine the poem being spoken by a character in a novel. What kind of life does he or she live?

9 The hope and forgiveness of the last line are 'unfounded conviction'. Consider the meaning of the phrase. Do you think the speaker of the poem is an optimistic or a pessimistic person? Do you agree with the views expressed by the speaker of the poem?

SEAMUS HEANEY

B. 1939

BIOGRAPHY

Seamus Heaney was born on 13 April, 1939, on a farm in County Derry. He was the eldest of nine children. He went to the local primary school and then to St Columb's College, a boarding school in Derry, about forty miles from his home. After St Columb's, Seamus won a scholarship to Queen's University, Belfast, where he studied English Literature and Language, graduating with a First Class Honours degree in 1961. He then trained as a teacher and got a job in a secondary school in Ballymurphy, Belfast. The principal teacher was Michael McLaverty, the short-story writer, who introduced Heaney to the work of Patrick Kavanagh. At about this time – 1962 – Heaney began to write poems in a serious way, and the poetry of Kavanagh influenced the direction and style of his work. Heaney wrote, 'Kavanagh gave you permission to dwell without cultural anxiety among the usual landmarks of your life'.

In August 1965, Seamus Heaney married Marie Devlin and in the following year, the London publishers Faber & Faber brought out his first collection of poems, *Death of a Naturalist*. Since then Heaney has published ten collections of poetry, five books of critical essays and a number of translations, including the Anglo-Saxon poem *Beowulf* which became an unlikely bestseller. With his friend, the late Ted Hughes, he has co-edited two poetry anthologies, *The Rattle Bag* and

The School Bag. His version of the Greek play *Antigone* was produced at the Abbey Theatre in 2004. Since *Death of a Naturalist* won the Eric Gregory prize in 1966, Seamus Heaney has won countless awards for his poetry. Winning the Nobel Prize for Literature in 1995 was an experience which he compared to being 'hit by a mostly benign avalanche'.

In 1976, Seamus Heaney and his family moved to Sandymount in Dublin. He now divides his time between living in Dublin and living in America and England, where he teaches and lectures at Harvard and Oxford.

At this point in his career, Seamus Heaney is, without question, one of the most admired poets writing in English. He is also a man of wit and high spirits who is modest about his achievements and who is still open to what he describes as 'the pleasure and surprise of poetry, its rightness and thereness, the way it is at one moment unforeseeable and at the next indispensable'.

POSTSCRIPT

And some time make the time to drive out west
Into County Clare, along the Flaggy Shore,
In September or October, when the wind
And the light are working off each other
So that the ocean on one side is wild   5
With foam and glitter, and inland among stones
The surface of a slate-grey lake is lit
By the earthed lightning of a flock of swans,
Their feathers roughed and ruffling, white on white,
Their fully-grown headstrong-looking heads   10
Tucked or cresting or busy underwater.
Useless to think you'll park and capture it
More thoroughly. You are neither here nor there,
A hurry through which known and strange things pass
As big soft buffetings come at the car sideways   15
And catch the heart off guard and blow it open.

GLOSSARY

title *Postscript*: something added as an afterthought

2 *the Flaggy Shore*: portion of the Atlantic shoreline near Finvarra County Clare, where the flat slabs of Burren limestone run right to the sea

11 *Tucked or cresting*: some of the swans have tucked in their heads so that they rest on their bodies; some have their necks extended while others have their heads underwater

15 *buffetings*: gusts of wind which push or knock against the car

GUIDELINES

Reading 'Postscript' is like overhearing the end of a conversation in which someone offers advice to a friend (or a tourist) to take a car journey along the west coast of Clare and describes the beauty of the journey and the feelings it inspires, especially in September or October.

The journey is a dramatic one, with the wild sea on one side and a lake on the other, upon which a flock of swans appear like 'earthed lightning'. Like a painter, the speaker appreciates the interplay between the light and the wind; the way the wind ruffles the feathers of the swans. Like everything else in this landscape the swans are powerful with 'fully-grown headstrong-looking heads'.

The poem has a sonnet-like structure in the division between description and reflection. The first eleven lines consist of the advice to 'make the time to drive out west' and a description of what lies in store. The last five lines are more reflective. In these lines the speaker suggests there is little point in stopping the car in hope of capturing the experience more fully. The sense of hurrying through the landscape, of being in motion and subject to the gusts of wind which catch the car sideways, is an essential part of the experience. The gusts of wind are not dangerous or threatening. On the contrary, they are 'big soft buffetings' which 'catch the heart off guard and blow it open'. In the last line the speaker seems to be referring to an experience of greater significance than the momentary heart-in-the-mouth experience of a wind catching a moving car and blowing it slightly off course.

Like all journey poems, 'Postscript' can be read in a metaphorical way. The journey symbolises to some degree the journey of life, especially at those moments when we seems to be 'neither here nor there' but exist on the edge of things, just as the car travels in the space between the land and the sea and is blown off balance. So the observation that it is 'Useless to think you'll park and capture it' might well be read as the speaker's philosophy that life cannot be controlled or commanded and our hearts will be blown open by the surprising and unexpected in our lives.

Interestingly, in introducing the poem at a reading Seamus Heaney spoke of the significance of 'going west' and his remarks might lead you to read the poem in a new light:

> The phrase, 'going west', from the First World War, has connotations of mortality, fatality, to 'go west'. And there's a very beautiful cadence in the last story of Joyce's Dubliners, 'The Dead', when Joyce says it was time for him to set out on his journey westward. So this is a memory of a vivid journey westward that we had.

QUESTIONS

1 The poem is rich in description. Select two images which you think are particularly effective and explain your choice.

2 Why, do you think, did Seamus Heaney decide to write the first eleven lines of description as one sentence?

3 Although conversational in tone, the poem has a feeling of strength about it. Examine the sounds of the poem and identify what you consider to be 'strong' sounds.

4 'A hurry through which known and strange things pass …'. In the overall context of the poem, what, do you think, is the meaning of this line?

5 'The speaker of the poem seems to enjoy the feeling of being off balance.' Do you agree with this statement? Explain your answer.

6 The poem reads like the advice of a wise man on how to lead your life. What is the wisdom that the speaker offers?

7 Why, in your opinion, is the poem entitled 'Postscript'? Does it suggest, for example, that the speaker is not claiming any great status for his advice and offers it modestly?

8 'The poem is written in ordinary language which seems to take flight and lifts off, just as the car seems to lift off as the wind catches it sideways.' Do you agree with this statement? Support your answer by reference to the poem.

9 Just as the phrase 'going west' strikes a chord in Heaney's imagination, the reference to swans on a lake is rich in connotations. What ideas does the image generate in your imagination?

10 Is the idea of a journey west a good metaphor for life? Explain your answer.

ELIZABETH JENNINGS

1926–2001

BIOGRAPHY

Elizabeth Jennings was born in Boston, Lincolnshire, the daughter of a physician. Roman Catholicism, the religion of her birth, was an important influence on her life and work. She read English at Oxford University, and afterwards worked in the Oxford Public Library. From the publication of her first collection of poems in 1953 onwards, her work won widespread critical acclaim. In the early 1960s, she suffered a severe nervous illness. The poems in her 1966 collection, the *Mind Has Mountains*, deal with her experiences in a psychiatric hospital. Before her illness, she worked in a publishing house in London. After her recovery, she continued to write poetry, as well as being a freelance critic, anthologist and lecturer on literary subjects.

Elizabeth Jennings found poetry an essential part of her life. Throughout her career, she remained a solitary person, relying on poetry as a vital link between her insecure private world and the seeming certainties of the world around her. Each poem could be seen as a temporary escape from isolation. There is an obsessive emphasis in her poetry on the theme of individual isolation. Some of her poems reveal a morbid fascination with the ultimate isolation – extinction in death. This poem from *Growing Points*, her 1975 collection, is a good example of this:

But better to be turned to earth
Where other things at least can grow,
I would be then a part of birth,
Passive, not knowing how to know.

Elizabeth Jennings was not an innovator. Her poetry has many of the character-
istics associated with the group of poets who belonged to what is commonly
known as 'the Movement'. Its members included Philip Larkin, Kingsley Amis,
Donald Davie, D. J. Enright, Thom Gunn and John Wain. Like the work of these
poets, hers displays a simplicity of metre and rhyme and a search for honest
feeling. Like them too, she was influenced by Thomas Hardy rather than by T. S.
Eliot, avoiding radical experiments in poetic forms.

THE LADYBIRD'S STORY

It was a roadway to me.
So many meeting-places and directions.
It was smooth, polished, sometimes it shook a little
But I did not tumble off.
I heard you say, and it was like a siren,   5
'A ladybird. Good luck. Perhaps some money.'
I did not understand.
Suddenly I was frightened, fearful of falling
Because you lifted your hand.

And then I saw your eyes,   10
Glassy moons always changing shape,
Sometimes suns in eclipse.
I watched the beak, the peak of your huge nose
And the island of your lips.
I was afraid but you were not. I have   15
No sting. I do not wound.
I carry a brittle coat. It does not protect.
I thought you would blow me away but superstition

Saved me. You held your hand now in one position,
Gentled me over the veins and arteries.   20
But it was not I you cared about but money.
You see I have watched you with flies.

GLOSSARY

17 *brittle*: frail and easily broken

20 *Gentled*: moved me gently

GUIDELINES

The entire poem is spoken by the ladybird to the poet. In form, the poem is a dramatic monologue. This is a work in which a single speaker dramatises an incident or situation, and derives significance or meaning from it.

The situation is simply presented. A ladybird finds itself on the poet's hand, and fears for its safety. To its relief, the poet treats it kindly, making sure that it comes to no harm.

The interest of the poem lies in the significance the ladybird derives from the situation and its outcome. From the ladybird's point of view, the poet is a representative human being, enormous in magnitude when compared to an insect. The human hand is a roadway to the ladybird, the eyes are moons and suns, the 'huge nose' is a beak, and the lips are an island. The ladybird knows that its fragile shell will provide no defence against hostile human intentions. It cannot fight against these, as some creatures can, by stinging or wounding the human enemy.

The ladybird is clever enough to realise, however, that human beings, as well as ladybirds, have their own weaknesses. In the present case, the weakness is superstition. The ladybird has heard the poet say, 'A ladybird. Good luck. Perhaps some money'. It also senses that this human being acts tenderly towards it, not out of a sympathy for small creatures, but out of a belief that saving it will bring monetary reward. It has observed this and other human beings killing flies without mercy, and knows that people in general have little regard for the welfare of insect life.

Jennings has written a thought-provoking poem as much about human nature as about a ladybird. Notice the bare simplicity of the language, and the conversational tone of the ladybird's song.

QUESTIONS

1 The poem indicates that the ladybird has mixed feelings about its experience. Develop this idea.
2 'The poet raises questions which extend far beyond a single incident.' Discuss this statement.
3 The poet uses imagery to express the ladybird's point of view on a human being. Discuss this imagery and say how effective it is.
4 Is the ladybird fair to the person it is dealing with?
5 Was it a good idea for the poet to present the situation from the ladybird's point of view? What advantages does this kind of presentation have?

PHILIP LARKIN

1922–85

BIOGRAPHY

Philip Larkin was born in Coventry in August 1922 into a middle-class family. He was the second child of Sydney and Eva Larkin. The family name is common in Ireland and it was often assumed that the poet had Irish ancestry. Larkin himself has no interest in family history but his father established that their branch of the family was English and had lived in the same part of the Midlands for generations.

Sydney Larkin was an accountant and, at the time of his son's birth, he was Treasurer of Coventry Corporation. He was well-read, agnostic in outlook and outspoken in his convictions. Eva, Larkin's mother, was intelligent but she was also nervous and timid and her husband ruled the household. There were constant tensions between Larkin's parents and this coloured his childhood, which he described as 'a forgotten boredom'. From an early age Larkin was ungainly and short-sighted. He was also shy and self-consciousness, so much so that, at age four, he developed a stammer.

By all accounts, the family home was a cold, lonely place. Because his sister, Kitty, was nine years older, Larkin felt like an only child. As he got older, his mother grew more anxious and nervous, his father more domineering and scornful, especially to Kitty, although he did communicate his love of literature and music to his son. Reviewing his parents' relationship in the 1950s, Larkin wrote: 'Certainly the marriage left me with two convictions: that human beings should not live together, and that children should be taken from their parents at an early age'. He also said that although he liked his parents, 'they were rather awkward people and not very good at being happy. And these things rub off.'

Larkin's father was an admirer of Hitler and German efficiency and he brought the teenage Philip on holiday to Germany in the 1930s. Later, Larkin said that these trips 'sowed the seed of my hatred of abroad'. In Germany, his natural shyness was intensified by his inability to speak the language and he was embarrassed by his father's enthusiasm for the National Socialists. As Larkin grew to manhood, he rejected all interest in politics although his outlook on life was decidedly conservative. From his father he inherited a 'total disbelief in Christianity'.

Larkin attended the local grammar school as his father despised the notion of elitist, private education. The school had a high academic standard and Larkin did well without excelling or wanting to excel. He made a number of close friends, one of whom, James Sutton, encouraged him to write and introduced him to jazz. In his final year, Larkin worked earnestly and wrote in a serious way. He was a regular contributor to the school magazine and acted as its assistant editor. Impressed by the improvement in his work, his English teacher suggested that he should study English at university. He took the entrance examination for St John's College, Oxford, in March 1940 and began his studies in autumn of that year. He read the poetry of W. H. Auden and his first poem, published as an undergraduate, reflects Auden's influence.

Philip Larkin spent three years at Oxford, from 1940 to 1943. Although the war curbed the activities of the students, Larkin enjoyed undergraduate life, adopting the pose of a dandy and listening to recordings of American jazz. It would be hard to overstate his love of jazz. He was intensely excited by it and many of his closest friends were fellow enthusiasts, including the young writer Kingsley Amis. Although dismissive of the set courses, Larkin read widely. Auden remained central to his view of literature and he admired Lawrence, Yeats (though he revised his opinion later) and Dylan Thomas. Above all, however, Larkin valued those writers who wrote without affectation and whose work remained close to ordinary, everyday life. Thomas Hardy embodied all that Larkin looked for in a poet.

Because of his poor eyesight, Larkin was not called up to the army. Fortunately none of his friends or close relatives was killed so Larkin was largely unaffected by the war and disinterested in its progress. In some respects Larkin was a flamboyant character at Oxford, but he still remained shy and self-conscious, especially with girls. The example of his father's unflattering opinion of women did little to help him overcome his awkwardness around members of the opposite sex.

With his friend and fellow writer, Kingsley Amis, Larkin developed a strong dislike of pomposity and a scathing, private disregard for 'respectability' that was to last a lifetime, although his public persona was polite and conformist.

As Larkin approached the end of his time in Oxford, he was sunk in depression. His writing was not progressing; the war had interrupted his friendships and his vexed relationships with women continued. Moreover, he had no idea of a career and seemed indecisive and passive as the time came for him to choose, a pattern that was to repeat itself at other, critical junctures in his life.

Much to his surprise and delight, Larkin got a First in his final exams. More surprisingly, returning to his parents' house from Oxford, his writing began to flow. Then he saw an advertisement for a librarian in a small town in the Midlands and decided to apply for it. His application was successful and he began work on 1 December, 1944. Although his letters reveal his initial dislike and contempt for the job, he soon began to enjoy the life of a librarian and found time for his writing. In 1945, his first collection of poetry, *The North Ship*, was published, by the small Fortune Press, which also published his novel *Jill* in 1946. This book describes, in fictional terms, Larkin's life as a student. Both the novel and the collection of poems met with muted responses. In 1947, Faber published Larkin's second novel, *A Girl in Winter*. It received favourable reviews and Larkin believed that he had begun his writer's life in earnest. In fact, he was to write no more fiction and produced only a small body of published work over his lifetime. However, he maintained a voluminous correspondence with his many friends. In his letters he presented different aspects of his personality to each of the correspondents. The letters, along with his diaries, reveal a complex personality and constitute an impressive and fascinating body of work.

During his time in Shropshire, Philip Larkin met and fell in love with a young girl, Ruth Bowman. To her, Larkin was witty, kind, outrageous and brilliant. To him, she was someone in whom he could confide and be himself. In 1948, when Larkin was 25 and struggling to come to terms with his father's death and his duty to his mother, he became engaged to Ruth, then aged 21. However, the omens were not good. In the first poems he wrote after they became lovers, Larkin dwelt on death. Furthermore, the prospect of marriage and the example of his parents' life together terrified Larkin, who was not prepared to give up his freedom or risk losing time for his writing. There was also the matter of his fear and stated dislike of children, for which he achieved a degree of notoriety. As with all the relationships in his life, Larkin failed to act decisively and the affair dragged on for two years before Ruth ended it.

Thereafter, Philip Larkin never married, though he was involved in two long-term relationships. One was with Monica Jones, a lecturer in the English Department at the University of Leicester, where Larkin worked for a short time. The other was with Maeve Brennan, a colleague of Larkin's whom he met in 1955 at the University of Hull.

In the summer of 1946, Larkin applied to and got a job in the library of University College, Leicester. The publication and success of *A Girl in Winter* brought him into contact with members of the academic staff and thus he met Monica Jones. But Larkin felt stifled by his life in Leicester and in 1950 he came to Belfast to work in the Library at Queen's University. Belfast freed Larkin from the pressures of personal relationships and family obligations. He enjoyed university life and conversation and he prepared his first major poetry collection, *The Less Deceived*, published by fledging publishing house The Marvell Press. In later years Larkin recalled that Belfast provided him with the best conditions for writing. He was surrounded by interesting and stimulating company; he had comfortable accommodation provided by the university; and he formed a number of romantic attachments that did not threaten him or impede his writing.

One of these attachments was for Winifred Arnott, a student and later a colleague of Larkin's at the library in Queen's. Her decision to marry and the departure of several close friends unsettled him. In 1955, he applied for the post of Librarian in the University of Hull. Larkin's quiet air of authority, his eloquence and the incisiveness of his mind impressed the interview board. They duly appointed him. During his time in Hull, the library underwent a transformation, growing from a staff of eleven to over one hundred. And while Larkin often spoke of his 'boring job', he took a professional pride in his stewardship of the library and was admired and respected within his profession. He personally oversaw the building of the new library in Hull and contributed many ideas to its design and decoration.

As Larkin established himself as a librarian, he won increasing recognition as a writer. *The Less Deceived* was highly successful, selling over 6,000 copies in the first years of publication and receiving favourable reviews. Selections of his poems appeared in all the major anthologies published in the late 1950s and early 1960s and he recorded a number of programmes for the BBC. He regularly reviewed poetry for *The Guardian* newspaper and became the jazz correspondent for the *Daily Telegraph*.

In a spirit of growing confidence, Larkin moved into a new flat in Hull in 1956 (and lived there until 1974.) Here he preserved his solitude, rarely inviting guests and keeping his work separate from his life as a writer. The intention was to create a space for his writing but the space often remained empty and he wrote less poetry than he had hoped to write. And all the while there was the conflict between his feelings for Maeve Brennan ('The woman I want to marry') and his loyalty to Monica Jones ('The woman I should marry') and the ambivalence of his attitude towards love and marriage.

Larkin's literary reputation was ensured with the publication of the collections *The Whitsun Weddings* (1964) and *High Windows* (1974), both of which were acclaimed as contemporary masterpieces. Awards and honours were heaped upon him, including a CBE in 1975. Following the publication of *The Whitsun Weddings*, he was invited to make a television programme for the BBC on his life and work, a project that gave him much delight and he made recordings of his poems. The Oxford University Press invited him to edit a new *Oxford Book of Modern Verse*, to replace the anthology edited by Yeats in 1936. (On its publication in 1973 it proved to be every bit as controversial as the original.) Larkin also served as a committee member for various poetry organisations using his administrative know-how to good effect. The student unrest of the 1960s brought out Larkin's reactionary prejudices. Students, trade unionists and immigrants were the targets of his acerbic wit.

As Philip Larkin grew older, he became somewhat reclusive. He disliked publicity, and enjoyed living in Hull, a long way from the centre of literary life in London. He liked to depict himself as a disgruntled, misanthropist, but friends testify to his humour and good companionship. In the last ten years of his life, Larkin wrote very little poetry. He believed that his inspiration had deserted him.The onset of deafness restricted his social activities, and deepened his frequent bouts of melancholy. His love-hate relationship with his family lasted right up to his mother's death in 1977, at the age of 91. In a letter he remarked that 'To escape from home is a life's work'. The economic cutbacks of the 1970s meant that the library in Hull was forced to curtail its services. To Larkin it seemed that everything was falling apart. By the age of fifty he had the mien of an old man and was gripped by bouts of remorse of feelings of failure. He described his situation in the opening verse of 'Aubade':

I work all day, and get half-drunk at night.
Waking at four to soundless dark, I stare.
In time the curtain edges will grow light.

Till then I see what's really there:
Unresting death, a whole day nearer now,
Making all thought impossible but how
And where and when I shall myself die.

Dispirited and melancholic, he turned to his closest friends and colleagues for support. The end of his days was marked by a sense of failure. He believed that he had set out to perfect his work and was left with only a failed life. Not even the offer to succeed John Betjeman as poet laureate, which he declined, cheered him. In June 1985, he was diagnosed as having cancer. After surgery and a short remission, he died in December, aged 63. His final words were 'I am going to the inevitable'. On his death, he was acclaimed as England's finest post-war poet, whose work transformed the contradictions, frustrations, fears and indignities of ordinary life into eloquent poetry.

SOCIAL AND CULTURAL CONTEXT

T. S. Eliot was the dominant figure in English poetry for the first third of the century. Eliot was a Modernist poet. Modernism arose out of the developments in psychoanalysis in the early part of the century and out of the crisis caused by the experience of the First World War. Psychoanalysis called into question our common-sense understanding of the world and the way we perceive it, while the war called standards of morality into question. To many, it seemed that the world was absurdly meaningless. In all areas of life, old forms had failed and new ones needed to be invented. Thus, as a movement, Modernism rejected traditional practices in favour of new techniques and experiments. Melody and harmony were abandoned in music, perspective and pictorial form rejected in art and linear narrative and argument were rejected in literature and replaced by new experimental forms. The result was an exciting kind of poetry, often fragmentary and random in its organisation – a poetry that was neither popular nor easily accessible.

As Europe went into recession in the late 1920s and Fascism rose in many countries, the experimentation of Modernism seemed indulgent to a generation of younger writers. Many of them were committed socialists. Their concern was to give expression to their political and social awareness and to speak to and for the poor and the working class within society. W. H. Auden became the leading figure in English poetry in the 1930s. For Auden, to be a writer was to be a citizen and to write was to put your insights at the service of your fellow citizens to give them strength to withstand their enemies. In some respects, Auden's view of poetry was shared by Larkin, who believed that poetry should help us to 'enjoy and endure'. However, Larkin was not interested in the political awareness that shaped Auden's work. For him, poetry was concerned with private, individual experience:

> I write about experiences, often quite simple, everyday experiences which somehow acquire some sort of special meaning for me, and I write poems about them to preserve them. You see, I want to express the experience in a poem so that it remains preserved, unchanging; and I then hope that other people will come upon this experience, pickled as it were in verse, and it will mean something to them, sound some chord in their own recollection, perhaps, or show them something familiar in a new light.

The first coherent development in poetry after the Second World War was The Movement – a loose grouping of poets who strove for clarity in their work and who used traditional forms in reaction against Modernism. The manifesto of The Movement was Robert Conquest's introduction to *New Lines*, an anthology he edited in 1956 in which he described the poets' refusal to abandon a rational structure and comprehensible language, even when the verse is most highly charged with sensuous or emotional intent.

For his part, Larkin rejected the example of T. S. Eliot in favour of the example of Thomas Hardy. Indeed, Larkin's work expresses nostalgia for the England evoked by Hardy, and Larkin admired the style of Hardy's writing, which is narrative, direct and personal. From Hardy's example, Larkin sought to explore the dilemmas of ordinary individuals in a language that was close to everyday speech and English in tone and manner. In a review of Hardy's collected poems, Larkin declared that it was the best body of poetic work the twentieth century so far had to show. Of course, this is not to say that Larkin's work does not reflect elements of the Modernist style or is simply an imitation of Hardy. Many of his own poems are complex and subtle, rich in symbolism and straining to go beyond the ordinary. In the words of the critic James Booth, Larkin strains language 'to the limits of grammatical tolerance'. However, it is true that Philip Larkin had little time for the experimentalism of Modernism or for poetry that was intellectually obscure. He admired poetry that was accessible and written with a keen sense of formality, using traditional verse patterns. He thought that life, as it was lived by ordinary people, should and could provide the subject of poetry. He wanted his poems to address a non-academic audience in the language of the everyday. Compared to the poetry of Ezra Pound or T. S. Eliot, Larkin succeeds in his ambitions.

Compared to the work of Modernist poets, Larkin makes few references to other poems or poets in his writing. Modernism was open to European and American influences and to the influence of the past. Larkin, however, disliked the idea that poems come from other poems. He believed that poems should arise from personal experience. (Of course, in discussing influence in poetry, everything is a matter of degree, for Larkin's poetry hints at other poets and poems, from Shakespeare to Keats, and his themes of death and transience are found in every major poet.) In Larkin's eyes, Modernism had destroyed the quality of delight that should accompany poetry: 'This is my essential criticism of modernism…it helps us neither to enjoy nor to endure.'

Larkin's life and career coincided with remarkable changes in English society. He lived through the Second World War and the economic depression of the 1950s. He was a librarian in Hull during the rapid expansion of the university system in England and the changes in attitude and culture brought about by the affluence of the 1960s. Student unrest in the late 1960s and early 1970s won no sympathy from him. Nor was he sympathetic to the increasingly multiracial nature of British society. His cure for unemployment was to stop unemployment benefit. As he grew older, he expressed alarmingly reactionary views in his private correspondence. In his final collection, *High Windows* (1974), there is a coarseness in some of the poems that is striking. He admired the leadership of Margaret Thatcher, though, ironically, it was the financial policies pursued by her government which led to the cutbacks in the university. These cutbacks undid many of Larkin's professional achievements.

These changes are almost totally absent from Larkin's poems. Whatever insights are won in his poetry arise from the observation of his own life and the ordinary lives around him. Perhaps it is only in the rueful tone of some poems in *High Windows*, where the persona of the poems envies the young their freedom, do we see the poetry reflecting public events.

THE EXPLOSION

On the day of the explosion
Shadows pointed towards the pithead:
In the sun the slagheap slept.

Down the lane came men in pitboots
Coughing oath-edged talk and pipe-smoke,   5
Shouldering off the freshened silence.

One chased after rabbits; lost them;
Came back with a nest of lark's eggs;
Showed them; lodged them in the grasses.

So they passed in beards and moleskins,   10
Fathers, brothers, nicknames, laughter,
Through the tall gates standing open.

At noon, there came a tremor; cows
Stopped chewing for a second; sun,
Scarfed as in a heat-haze, dimmed.   15

The dead go on before us, they
Are sitting in God's house in comfort,
We shall see them face to face –

Plain as lettering in the chapels
It was said, and for a second   20
Wives saw men of the explosion

Larger than in life they managed –
Gold as on a coin, or walking
Somehow from the sun towards them,

One showing the eggs unbroken.   25

GLOSSARY

2 *pithead*: the top of the mine shaft and the various buildings around it

3 *slagheap*: the hill or mound made of the waste material from coal mining

10 *moleskins*: a hard-wearing cotton used for work clothes. Miners wore moleskin trousers to work

16–18 *The dead … face-to-face*: the verse is taken from a prayer from the funeral service. These words formed part of the vision of the wives

GUIDELINES

The poem was written over Christmas in 1969. It appeared in *High Windows* (1971). The poem presents an account of a mine explosion in which many miners lost their lives. It was reported that, at the moment of the explosion, the wives of the miners had visions of their husbands. The source of the poem was a television documentary on the mining industry that Larkin watched with his mother. It may also have been influenced by his rereading of the work of D. H. Lawrence.

The poem is unusual in that there is no 'I' persona to supply the customary Larkin perspective on the events described. Instead, 'The Explosion' is a poem of observation and takes its tone from the event itself.

The first stanza paints a quiet scene, but there are hints of the disaster to come in the references to shadows and the sleeping slagheap. In the second stanza, the miners are portrayed as rough and ready as they make their way to the pithead. In Stanza Three, a miner, hurrying after the rabbit and returning with a nest of lark's eggs, alerts us the vitality in these men, and their closeness to nature. The fourth stanza suggests the close-knit community of the pit workers: fathers and sons, and friends and companions, laughing together as they pass through 'the tall gates standing open'. The image of the gates suggest the entry into death's kingdom. The long vowel sound of this stanza create an elegiac tone, as if the poet wishes to rouse our sympathy for these innocent men marching towards their death, without a care or an intimation of what is to come.

In Stanza Five, the explosion is registered on the surface by a mere tremor. This stanza suggests that, much as we might wish it otherwise, sudden death does not stop the flow of life. However, the poem seeks to register the deaths of these men, and the vision of the wives is used to give the poem a remarkably uplifting ending, in the final, floating, line with its suggestion of Easter eggs and resurrection: 'One showing the eggs unbroken'.

In 'The Explosion', Larkin is back to the 'almost-instinct' of 'An Arundel Tomb', that what will survive of us is love. The poem does not declare that the men are transformed by death, but that they are transformed in the visions of their wives. This final, optimistic image contains a suggestion of continuity and generation. The poem, without stating anything directly, offers a testament to the power of love to withstand tragedy and death.

QUESTIONS

1 From as early as the first stanza, the poem hints at the disaster to come. How is this done? Where else, in the first four stanzas, are there intimations of disaster?

2 Between Stanzas Two and Four, Larkin deftly sketches the community of pit workers. What do we learn of the men and their relationship to each other?

3 One miner discovers a nest of lark's eggs. He lodges them in the grasses. Why does he do this? What is the point of this detail in relation to the impending disaster and the theme of the poem?

4 The sixth stanza consists of an extract from the funeral service. Is the tone and rhythm of this stanza in keeping with the rest of the poem?

5 How does the poem deal with the reported visions of the wives of the explosion? What is the poem's attitude to death and suffering?

6 The final four stanzas are difficult to read, both in terms of syntax and grammar. Attempt a paraphrase of the stanzas, supplying missing words where needed. What, in your view, is lost or gained in paraphrasing the lines?

7 The poem ends with an image of unbroken eggs. This image contains a suggestion of both continuity and generation. What does this line contribute to your understanding of the theme of the poem?

8 What similarities in theme and attitude can you find between this poem and 'An Arundel Tomb' in relation to marriage and death?

AT GRASS

The eye can hardly pick them out
From the cold shade they shelter in,
Till wind distresses tail and mane;
Then one crops grass, and moves about
– The other seeming to look on –   5
And stands anonymous again.

Yet fifteen years ago, perhaps
Two dozen distances sufficed
To fable them: faint afternoons
Of Cups and Stakes and Handicaps,   10
Whereby their names were artificed
To inlay faded, classic Junes –

Silks at the start: against the sky
Numbers and parasols: outside,
Squadrons of empty cars, and heat,   15
And littered grass: then the long cry
Hanging unhushed till it subside
To stop-press columns on the street.

Do memories plague their ears like flies?
They shake their heads. Dusk brims the shadows.   20
Summer by summer all stole away,
The starting-gates, the crowds and cries –
All but the unmolesting meadows.
Almanacked, their names live; they

Have slipped their names, and stand at ease,   25
Or gallop for what must be joy,
And not a fieldglass sees them home,
Or curious stop-watch prophesies:
Only the groom, and the groom's boy,
With bridles in the evening come.   30

GLOSSARY

3 *distresses*: ruffles or upsets. The word may suggest the nervousness of thoroughbred horses

4 *crops*: grazes or eats the grass

8 *Two dozen distances*: two dozen races or the distance of the race itself. (A distance' is a point 240 yards back from the winning post.)

9 *fable*: to make famous in the lore of racing

10 *Cups and Stakes and Handicaps*: types of horse races

11 *their names were artificed / To inlay classic Junes*: Larkin takes a noun (artifice') and turns it into a verb. The formal, registered names of the horses were made fancy ('artificed') to decorate or ornament (inlay') the important ('classic') races of the season. These races were held in June and have now 'faded' from memory

13 *Silks*: the colourful garments worn by jockeys

23 *unmolesting*: the implied contrast is between the meadows and the crowds who swarm around the winning horse at the end of an important race

24 *Almanacked*: here, as in many of his poems, Larkin plays with words. He transforms the noun 'almanack' into a verb. An almanack is an annual calendar, giving information of particular topics. In this case, the verb means 'recorded in the racing records'

25 *slipped*: to be let loose from. Larkin plays with the idea of horses being freed from their bridles. The horses are freed from their racing names and the obligation to race

28 *stop-watch prophesies*: the prospects of young race horses are determined by the times they register on the stop watch

GUIDELINES

Larkin wrote this poem in 1950. It appeared in *The Less Deceived* (1955).

The idea for 'At Grass' came to Larkin after he attended the cinema and saw a documentary on a retired racehorse. The film made a deep impression on the poet.

The poem begins in a quiet, undramatic manner and captures the visual quality of the documentary that inspired the poem. However, the vocabulary hints at themes beyond the level of description. The phrase 'the cold shade' suggests death, and sets up an expectation that this meditation on the retired horses will involve an apprehension of death. The first line, 'The eye can hardly pick them out', suggests that the horses are becoming indistinct as, in the words of one critic, 'their fame recedes and their death approaches'.

In the second stanza, we get an idea of Larkin's richly-layered poetic method. Picking up on the idea of distance – the distance of the horses from the poet and the distance of the horses from their former lives – the poet thinks of the distances the horses ran to bring them into racing history. The final two lines of the stanza suggest the formal, registered names of the racehorses, as well as the inscription of the winning horse's name on racing trophies. The lines also contain the suggestion that horse racing, itself, is a kind of rich ornamentation or inlay to social life.

In Stanza Three Larkin uses a cinematic effect to evoke the fashion, wealth, hope, expectation and media interest that surrounds horse-racing in England. The opening of Stanza Four is whimsical. The horses shake their head in answer to the question posed in the first line: 'Do memories plague their ears like flies? / They shake their heads'. The lines bring into focus a major theme of the poem. However much human beings use horses for their sporting purposes, the horses themselves remain outside any understanding of that world. The racing names live on in the records of racing annuals, but the horses themselves 'have slipped their names' and have returned to 'the unmolesting meadows'. The fourth and fifth stanzas imply that the horses, now in the twilight of their lives, are free of the unwelcome attention of humans.

The ending of the poem is beautifully achieved. The horses' names and their fame will live long after they have died. The thought of the final line of stanza four is left incomplete: 'Almanacked, their names live; they ... [will die]'. But before death comes, there is the freedom of the days at grass. Now the horses gallop 'for what must be joy', away from the watchful eyes of racegoers. The final two lines take on an emotional resonance through the mellow-sounding phrases and the alliteration. The poetic effect is heightened by the inversion of the word order. The effect is to create a fine sense of closure, as the groom and the groom's boy come to take in the horses:

> Only the groom, and the groom's boy,
> With bridles in the evening come.

The ending suggests the final homecoming of horses whose lives have been safely and successfully concluded.

Larkin's biographer, Andrew Motion relates 'At Grass' to the personal crisis through which the poet was living. Larkin had yet to come to terms with the death of his father. His relationship with Ruth Bowman was coming to an end, and his relationship with his mother was beset by guilt and frustration. In these circumstances, the situation of the horses was to be envied.

QUESTIONS

1 The opening stanza of the poem is quiet and undramatic. What words or phrases hint at themes beyond the level of description?

2 The first stanza suggests the distance of the horses from the observer. The concept of distance runs through the poem. What other types of distances are explored in 'At Grass'?

3 In Stanza Three the world of racing is suggested in a series of cinematic images. What kind of world emerges from these images?

4 The phrase 'unmolesting meadows' is a startling one. What does it contribute to the reader's understanding of the poem's themes?

5 The final stanza is rich and complex. Explain how the images, language and rhythm suggest both freedom and the approach of death.

6 Some critics read 'At Grass' as expressing Larkin's nostalgia for an England that is disappearing. Others read it as expressing Larkin's personal sense of loss at the ending of his engagement to Ruth Bowman. Can you find evidence in the poem to support either of these readings?

7 What, in your opinion, are the main themes of 'At Grass'?

AN ARUNDEL TOMB

Side by side, their faces blurred,
The earl and countess lie in stone,
Their proper habits vaguely shown
As jointed armour, stiffened pleat,
And that faint hint of the absurd –   5
The little dogs under their feet.

Such plainness of the pre-baroque
Hardly involves the eye, until
It meets his left-hand gauntlet, still
Clasped empty in the other; and   10
One sees, with a sharp tender shock,
His hand withdrawn, holding her hand.

They would not think to lie so long.
Such faithfulness in effigy
Was just a detail friends would see: 15
A sculpture's sweet commissioned grace
Thrown off in helping to prolong
The Latin names around the base.

They would not guess how early in
Their supine stationary voyage   20
The air would change to soundless damage,
Turn the old tenantry away;
How soon succeeding eyes begin
To look, not read. Rigidly they

Persisted, linked, through lengths and breadths   25
Of time. Snow fell, undated. Light
Each summer thronged the glass. A bright
Litter of birdcalls strewed the same
Bone-riddled ground. And up the paths
The endless altered people came,   30

Washing at their identity.
Now, helpless in the hollow of
An unarmorial age, a trough
Of smoke in slow suspended skeins
Above their scrap of history,   35
Only an attitude remains:

Time has transfigured them into
Untruth. The stone fidelity
They hardly meant has come to be
Their final blazon, and to prove   40
Our almost-instinct almost true:
What will survive of us is love.

GLOSSARY

7 *pre-Baroque*: Baroque is a style of art and architecture that flourished in the
   seventeenth century. It is characterised by elaborate ornamentation. Pre-Baroque
   suggests a style of art that is plain and free from ornamentation

9 *gauntlet*: the glove in a suit of armour

14 effigy: a sculpted likeness or a portrait used in a monument

16 *grace*: goodwill or kindness or elegance

20 *supine*: the word describes the pose of the sculptured earl and countess who lie
   on their backs with their faces upwards

22 *tenantry*: the tenants of an estate

33 *unarmorial age*: the post-medieval period, or an age that has no concern for social
   distinctions based upon the status of a family. 'Armorial' relates to heraldry i.e.
   coats of arms and genealogies

34 *skeins*: the usual meaning is a length of thread or yarn. It also can refer to a lock
   of hair, or here, wisps of smoke

40 *blazon*: coat of arms or symbol. It also has the meaning of a public statement
   or proclamation

GUIDELINES

The poem was written in 1956 following a holiday visit to Chichester Cathedral in the company of Monica Jones. Larkin had spent time nursing his mother who had been seriously ill, and he had worries about his own state of health. The poem is a meditation on transience, death and the survival of love. 'An Arundel Tomb' appeared in *The Whitsun Weddings* (1964).

The poem is a meditation on the notion of the permanence of love and the strong hope and desire that humans have that love will remain – a hope which Larkin refers to as 'Our almost-instinct'. The Arundel tomb, featuring sculptured effigies of the Earl of Arundel and his wife, is a reminder of the inevitability of death and yet, in the clasped hands of the reclining figures, the tomb stands as a monument to enduring, faithful love.

In 'An Arundel Tomb' there is a clear conflict between the emotional force of the poem, which wants to proclaim 'What will survive of us is love' and the intellectual honesty, which denies the truth of this sentiment and declares: 'Time has transfigured them into untruth'. It is a familiar tension in Larkin's work.

The meditation on the tomb, and on the passing of time, is both aware of and alert to the ironic transformation which the tomb has undergone. The poem recognises that the contemporary meaning of the tomb is at odds with the original purpose that the monument was intended to serve. The tomb now expresses a meaning that neither the earl and countess nor the sculptor could have envisaged.

Now the couple serve as an emblem of faithful, tender love, an English version of Romeo and Juliet. The lesson that the speaker takes from this is that we, too, are subject to time. We have little control over the meaning of our lives after we have gone. And while the tomb stands as an emblem of love's survival, the individual identities of the earl and his countess have been washed away. What remains of them is the sculptured pose.

The poem points out an illusion of art – the illusion that art can preserve meaning and hold back time. But this is not so. The original intention of the tomb was to keep alive the names of the dead, to honour important people. Yet what remains is the gesture of affection and tenderness, the hands clasped in each other's, although we have no way of knowing if the couple were the devoted lovers suggested by this gesture. A deeper irony is that, unknown to Larkin when he wrote the poem, the gesture upon which the poem depends is a late addition. It was added to the effigies some four hundred years after the burial of the earl and the countess during restoration work in the cathedral in the 1840s.

It is possible to read a poem as a meditation on falsehood. The gesture of affection is simply a lie and the poem reveals Larkin's doubts about the possibility of a long-lasting relationship. Read in this way, the last two lines indicate Larkin's belief that no living couple could ever be truly happy and remain permanently in love.

Andrew Motion provides an interesting insight into Larkin's attitude to his own achievement in 'An Arundel Tomb'. He tells us that:

> At the end of the manuscript draft of 'An Arundel Tomb' Larkin wrote, 'Love isn't stronger than death just because statues hold hands for 600 years'. It is a remark which reinforced, privately, the sense of futility that hovers around the poem's conclusion in words like 'helpless', 'scrap', 'attitude', 'Untruth' and 'almost' (and it typifies his habit of writing cynical graffiti on his own most monumental lines.)

QUESTIONS

1 What is the tone of the opening stanza: detached, disinterested, amused, superior? Perhaps you could suggest another term.

2 '…a sharp tender shock …' (line 11). This is a key moment in the poem. How does the phrase succeed in drawing attention to itself? How does Larkin convey the tenderness of the gesture in the language of the final line of Stanza Two? Select other examples of lines where there is a successful blending of sound and sense.

3 The gesture of fidelity is now what gives meaning to the monument. What does the speaker suggest, in Stanza Three, was the original significance of the gesture of the earl holding the hand of his wife?

4 How, throughout the poem, and in particular in the fourth and fifth stanzas, does the poet convey the idea that the monument serves less and less as a commemoration of two individuals?

5 What purpose does the monument now serve?

6 What is the effect of the verb 'begin' in line 23? What potential difficulties are there in reading Stanza Four in terms of grammar and syntax?

7 There is a brilliant evocation of the passage of time, beginning in the last line of Stanza Five and continuing into the first line of Stanza Seven. Examine each of the images in this passage and comment on their effectiveness. How does the rhythm of these lines form part of their meaning?

8 'The endless altered people.' In what way are the people altered? There is clearly a pun on the words alter/altar. Explain it.

9 The lives and feelings of earl and the countess are gone. Now, all that remains is 'a trough of smoke ... above their scrap of history'. What, do you think, is the speaker's attitude towards the loss of their identity?

10 The final stanza begins with the grave and dignified statement: 'Time has transfigured them into untruth'. What is the untruth? Is the untruth of the monument a beautiful untruth? Does it fill a need in us? Is the poem suggesting here that art is a form of self-delusion?

DEREK MAHON

B. 1941

BIOGRAPHY

Derek Mahon was born on 23 November, 1941 in Belfast and brought up in the suburb of Glengormley. His father was an engine-inspector in the Belfast shipyard of Harland and Wolff, where both his grandfathers had also been employed, while his mother worked for a time in York St Flax Spinning Company. As he himself has said, his parents thus 'embodied the two principal industries in Northern Ireland, ship-building and linen'.

Although Mahon's own background was working-class Protestant, Mahon played as a child with Catholic children, Glengormley being a mixed neighbourhood. He describes himself in one of his poems as having been 'A strange child with a taste for verse'. He went to secondary school at the Royal Belfast Academical Institution. The poet Michael Longley was a contemporary of his at the school and remembers him as already being an accomplished poet at this time.

Like Longley, Mahon went on to study at Trinity College, Dublin. He studied modern languages there, specialising in French, but also began to work seriously at the craft of poetry. Mahon was part of a group of other gifted young poets studying at TCD at the time: Eavan Boland, Brendan Kennelly and Michael Longley. For the first time Mahon felt that there was a poetry-writing community that he could be part of, as well as a thriving literary scene in Dublin.

After taking his BA in Trinity College, Mahon studied at the Sorbonne in Paris. He worked as a teacher in the USA, Canada and Ireland before becoming a journalist and writer in London. He was theatre critic for *The Listener* for a time, poetry editor for *The New Statesman*, and features editor of *Vogue* magazine. He was also involved in adapting Irish novels for television, among them Jennifer Johnston's *How Many Miles to Babylon?*, as well as radio adaptations and features. He was writer-in-residence at New University of Ulster 1978–79, and at TCD in 1988. He has been a regular contributor of literary journalism and book reviews to *The Irish Times*.

For several years in the 1990s Mahon lived in New York where he taught at New York University. Having by this time divorced his wife Doreen Douglas, whom he married in 1972, much of his work from New York was addressed to his two children, Rory and Katie, with whom he was no longer living. By 1996 he had returned to live in Dublin.

Poems 1962–78 brings together most of the poems from his first three collections, *Night Crossing* (1968), *Lives* (1972) and *The Snow Party* (1975). *Courtyards in Delft* appeared in 1981, *The Hunt by Night* in 1983, and *Antarctica* in 1985. *Selected Poems* (1991) was the winner of the *Irish Times*-Aer Lingus Irish Literature Prize for Poetry in 1992.

Derek Mahon has also edited some poetry anthologies and published several verse translations, including Moliere's *School for Wives*, the poems of Philippe Jaccottet from the French and a version of *The Bacchae* by the Greek Euripides.

A member of Aosdána and a fellow of the Royal Society of Literature, he has received numerous awards, among them the American Ireland Literary Award and the C. K. Scott- Moncrieff prize for translation.

In 1999 he published his *Collected Poems*, with updated versions of many of the poems he has written during the course of his distinguished career. His latest collection is *Harbour Lights* (2005).

SOCIAL AND CULTURAL CONTEXT

Derek Mahon once said in an interview that he considers himself to be a European poet who happens to be Irish, and who also just happens to have been born in Belfast. Each of the three strands of his chosen cultural identity has its place in the development of his work.

As a poet from Northern Ireland his work responds in a complex way to the society into which he was born. He is acutely aware of his roots, as the poem 'Grandfather' suggests, revealing a certain admiration for traits that have been associated with the Northern Irish character, such as a certain rebelliousness and self-reliance. On the other hand, in a poem such as 'Ecclesiastes' he rejects the bigoted attitudes of the churchmen of his native Belfast – a rejection that is tinged with admission of the attractions of that way of life. He has never sought to engage with the political problems or the conflict in Northern Ireland. He once said that he felt that poets in Ulster are 'supposed to write about the Troubles; a lot of people expect us to act as if it were part of our job – it's not, unless we choose to make it so'.

And yet it is true to say that Mahon does not flinch from confronting the issue of violence, even if in a rather oblique way. The lesson of history is an important theme in his poems, and his attitude to the questions that have caused much grief in Ireland can be seen from his statement that 'whatever we mean by the "Irish situation", the shipyards of Belfast are no less a part of it than a country town in the Gaeltacht'.

Mahon's education at Trinity College Dublin widened his cultural experience. In the 1960s students at Trinity College were predominantly Protestant since Catholics were forbidden to attend. Mahon, however, met several Southern Irish Catholic students at the university, among them the Kerry poet Brendan Kennelly and the Dublin poet Eavan Boland. Having lived in Dublin while attending college and for some time afterward, Mahon became familiar with life in the south of Ireland, which he may not have done had he remained in Belfast. An abiding love for the landscape of the west of Ireland is shown in his poems about Inis Oirr, Achill and Donegal.

Mahon's assimilation of French literature at university led to his translations of classical French texts and modern French poetry. As a student in Paris, Mahon met the Irish dramatist Samuel Beckett , who, like himself, had been educated at Trinity. Like Beckett, Mahon's self-induced exile enabled him to write of his native country as an observer rather than as a participant in the Irish cultural scene. Many of his poems reflect also an interest in European art. He is conscious of the complex link between poetry and painting that is so important in his work. His imagery is frequently concerned with the effects of light and shade, as an artist would be.

Derek Mahon has lived in the USA and some of his poems describe the American landscape and way of life. Although he has returned to Ireland, his poetic vision continues to be truly international. His themes are universal. His frame of reference and allusions contain many diverse cultural echoes. He has expressed the view that for him poetry is primarily an artistic activity rather than an expression of a particular cultural identity: 'for me, poetry is about shape and sound. It's about taking the formless and making it interesting; creating art out of formlessness.'

GRANDFATHER

They brought him in on a stretcher from the world,
Wounded but humorous; and he soon recovered.
Boiler-rooms, row upon row of gantries rolled
Away to reveal the landscape of a childhood
Only he can recapture. Even on cold   5
Mornings he is up at six with a block of wood
Or a box of nails, discreetly up to no good
Or banging round the house like a four-year-old—

Never there when you call. But after dark
You hear his great boots thumping in the hall   10
And in he comes, as cute as they come. Each night
His shrewd eyes bolt the door and set the clock
Against the future, then his light goes out.
Nothing escapes him; he escapes us all.

GLOSSARY

3 *gantries*: overhead platform for a travelling crane used in shipbuilding

GUIDELINES

'Grandfather' is from the collection *Night Crossing* (1968).

Derek Mahon's grandfather was a boiler-maker in Harland and Wolff, the ship-builders in Belfast where the *Titanic* was built. In this sonnet the poet paints an interesting portrait of the old man.

In the first eight lines, the octet, we see the old man as an outsider, isolated from the real world but living his own rich life. Images of his working life recede as he seems to recapture the freedom of childhood. Mahon's wry humour evokes a picture of a harmless old man.

The sestet offers a slightly different perspective on the grandfather, however. The colloquial phrase 'as cute as they come' suggests that his actions are far from aimless. Perhaps he has found a way to avoid confronting the problems of real life. Certainly we are left with an impression of an old man who has stubbornly refused to adapt to the conventions of 'normal' elderly behaviour.

QUESTIONS

1 What do the first two lines of the poem convey to you about the grandfather? Is this initial impression borne out by the rest of the poem?

2 Why do you think the poet refers to his grandfather's working life? Is this significant in the poem, in your view?

3 Look at the colloquial phrases 'up to no good', 'as cute as they come', and the similes and metaphors used to describe the old man. What do they contribute to our sense of the sort of person he is?

4 Is there another view of the grandfather suggested in the sestet? Look in particular at the last three lines.

5 Which of these words best describes the grandfather, as he is presented in the poem: mysterious, eccentric, innocent, doddering, rebellious, clever? Perhaps you would suggest another word?

6 How would you describe Mahon's attitude to his grandfather?

7 Using poetic means, Mahon has given us a vivid picture of his grandfather. Write a short descriptive portrait of the most interesting person you know.

AFTER THE TITANIC

They said I got away in a boat
And humbled me at the inquiry. I tell you
    I sank as far that night as any
Hero. As I sat shivering on the dark water
    I turned to ice to hear my costly   5
Life go thundering down in a pandemonium of
    Prams, pianos, sideboards, winches,
Boilers bursting and shredded ragtime. Now I hide
    In a lonely house behind the sea
Where the tide leaves broken toys and hat-boxes   10
    Silently at my door. The showers of
April, flowers of May mean nothing to me, nor the
    Late light of June, when my gardener
Describes to strangers how the old man stays in bed
    On seaward mornings after nights of   15
Wind, takes his cocaine and will see no-one. Then it is
    I drown again with all those dim
Lost faces I never understood. My poor soul
    Screams out in the starlight, heart
Breaks loose and rolls down like a stone.   20
    Include me in your lamentations.

GLOSSARY

6 *pandemonium*: chaos, confusion

7 *winches*: machinery used to lift heavy goods

8 *ragtime*: the popular jazz music that was played by the ship's orchestra as it was sinking

21 *lamentations*: mourning. There is also a book of the Old Testament called 'The Lamentations of Jeremiah'

This poem comes from the collection *Lives* (1975).

In April 1912 The *SS Titanic* struck an iceberg off the coast of Newfoundland and sank with the loss of almost 1,500 lives. After the tragedy, an inquiry was held into the disaster. Among those questioned was Bruce Ismay, the President of White Star Line (the ship's owners), one of the few male passengers who had managed to escape in the lifeboats. In this dramatic monologue, Derek Mahon gives a voice to Bruce Ismay. The poem was in fact originally entitled 'Bruce Ismay's Soliloquy'.

The *Titanic* had been built in Belfast, at the Harland and Wolff shipyard. Perhaps the fact that Mahon's own grandfather was a boiler-maker for the ship (the poem contains a reference to boilers bursting) inspired the poet to reconstruct the events and enter imaginatively into the mind of the speaker.

Even though he distances himself from the verdict of the inquiry, Bruce Ismay wants to convince himself (and his listeners) that he, too, was a victim of the tragedy. In vivid images he evokes the atmosphere of chaos as the ship was sinking. Then he describes how he lives his life in the aftermath of the disaster. Feeling ashamed and guilty, he hides away from the world. Ironically, he has chosen to live by the sea, where the detritus left by the tide seems further to accuse him.

The metaphors and similes in the last few lines convey feelings of utter desolation. He suffers emotionally and physically. Although we can detect a note of self-pity here, the speaker seeks to justify why he too should be included in any 'lamentations' or expressions of grief for those who suffered.

QUESTIONS

1 Why do you think the speaker of this poem feels compelled to give his side of the story?

2 What might he mean when he says 'I turned to ice to hear my costly / Life go thundering down ...'? Does what he says later help to explain it further?

3 Does he paint a vivid picture of the disaster, in your view?

4 Do you find it strange that he has chosen to live out his days beside the sea? Why might he have made this decision?

5 From the list of phrases that follow, choose one that is closest to your own reading of the poem and explain your choice:

a) This man is trying to justify his own cowardly actions.

b) This speaker feels genuinely sorry for what he has done.

c) This speaker has suffered greatly — it would have been better for him to have drowned like the others.

6 What does the speaker of the poem reveal about his personality? Do you find him a sympathetic character?

7 Examine the sound effects of the poem (alliteration, onomatopoeia, assonance). What do they contribute to its overall impact?

8 Would you agree that the dramatic monologue succeeds in conveying several points of view at once? Explain your view.

9 The poem evokes the disaster and its aftermath in an imaginative way. The speaker also refers to the inquiry. Using the language of information, write an account of the inquiry. (You need not base your account on historical facts only.)

10 Do you like this poem? Give reasons for your opinion.

ANTARCTICA

(for Richard Ryan)

'I am just going outside and may be some time.'
The others nod, pretending not to know.
At the heart of the ridiculous, the sublime.

He leaves them reading and begins to climb,
Goading his ghost into the howling snow;   5
He is just going outside and may be some time.

The tent recedes beneath its crust of rime
And frostbite is replaced by vertigo:
At the heart of the ridiculous, the sublime.

Need we consider it some sort of crime,   10
This numb self-sacrifice of the weakest? No,
He is just going outside and may be some time—

In fact, for ever. Solitary enzyme,
Though the night yield no glimmer there will glow,
At the heart of the ridiculous, the sublime.   15

He takes leave of the earthly pantomime
Quietly, knowing it is time to go.
'I am just going outside and may be some time.'
At the heart of the ridiculous, the sublime.

title *Antarctica*: the Antarctic is the South polar region

dedication *for Richard Ryan*: Richard Ryan is an Irish diplomat and poet

3 *sublime*: noble, awe-inspiring

5 *goading*: urging on

7 *rime*: frost

8 *frostbite*: damage to body tissue exposed to freezing temperatures

8 *vertigo*: dizziness, tendency to lose balance

13 *enzyme*: an enzyme is a protein that causes a living organism to change but is not changed itself

GUIDELINES

This poem comes from the collection *Antarctica* (1985). It is dedicated to the poet Richard Ryan.

In 1912 the explorer Captain Scott led an expedition to the South Pole, but he and his men perished in the attempt. In the diary found after his death, Scott describes how one of the men, Captain Oates, sacrificed himself in order to save food for the others by crawling out into a blizzard, saying only 'I am just going out and may be some time'. The words have become famous as examples of understatement and a certain kind of heroism.

Derek Mahon dramatises the incident in a villanelle that matches beautifully the dignity of Oates's last grim resolve. Oates's words open the poem and form one of the two refrains used in the poem. In exploring the implications of these words, Mahon is writing from a modern perspective where extreme heroic gestures have become more rare and even slightly suspect. We can see how he might suggest that the words are ridiculous in their failure to register even the smallest amount of emotion and their glaring understatement. As we know, 'some time' means, in fact, for ever.

On the other hand, the poet acknowledges the 'sublime' aspect of the event too – the nobility and unselfishness with which Oates acted. As Oates climbs to his death, he is depicted in images of suffering and endurance that lend dignity to his famous words.

The poem then questions present-day attitudes to such sacrifices. Oates is finally depicted, metaphorically, as a 'solitary enzyme' that will glow in the night. He knew the right thing to do and when to do it. The refrain, ending finally with the word 'sublime', now appears as a tribute.

The form of the poem is a villanelle. It is said to have a singing line. There is a sequence of tercets (three lines), with rhyming scheme aba, aba, aba in each. Each tercet ends in a refrain, and there are only two refrains alternating throughout the poem. The set of tercets is rounded off with a quatrain in which the two refrains at last come together, one capping the other. A villanelle is a highly stylised, formal poem that has become associated with meditations on death or grief.

QUESTIONS

1 Why do you think the words 'I am just going out and may be some time' could be seen as ridiculous? Why are they also sublime?

2 What picture of the members of the expedition do you get from reading this poem?

3 What sort of person was Oates, as suggested in the poem?

4 What do you think the poet is suggesting when he asks 'Need we consider it some sort of crime / This numb self-sacrifice of the weakest?'

5 Does the poem celebrate heroism, or does it have an ironic attitude to it?

6 What attitude to life and death is suggested by 'Antarctica'?

7 What is your own response to the issues raised in the poem?

ROGER McGOUGH

B. 1937

BIOGRAPHY

Roger McGough was born in Liverpool. He has married twice and has three sons and one daughter. He received his higher education at Hull University. He is a poet, dramatist, songwriter and performer. He was one of the group, along with Brian Patten and Adrian Henri, which became popularly known as 'The Liverpool Poets'. He became famous in the late 1960s as a member of the pop group Scaffold, and wrote many of their songs, including 'Lily the Pink' (1968). His poems were strongly influenced by the pop culture of the 1960s (the Mersey beat), and by the poets of the American Beat Generation. With his fellow-poets Brian Patten and Adrian Henri, McGough published the highly successful *Mersey Sound* poetry collection in 1967. His collections include *Gig* (1973) and *Waving at Trains* (1982). One of his fellow band members in Scaffold was Mike McCartney, whose brother Paul played in the world's most famous band, The Beatles.

McGough has written for theatre, film and television, and continues to write poetry: his latest collection, *Everyday Eclipses*, was published in 2002. His work has been widely translated. He is an international ambassador for poetry, and was awarded an OBE for his work in 1997. In 2001, he was made a freeman of the City of Liverpool. Much of his poetry has been written for live performances, which helps to explain why it is easily understood. The fact that it deals with the experiences and hopes of ordinary people has made it widely popular. It has a considerable appeal to children, since McGough speaks their language and understands their concerns and interests. This explains its widespread use in schools.

BEARHUGS

Whenever my sons call round we hug each other.
Bearhugs. Both bigger than me and stronger
They lift me off my feet, crushing the life out of me.

They smell of oil paint and aftershave, of beer
Sometimes and tobacco, and of women   5
Whose memory they seem reluctant to wash away.

They haven't lived with me for years,
Since they were tiny, and so each visit
Is an assessment, a reassurance of love unspoken.

I look for some resemblance to my family.   10
Seize on an expression, a lifted eyebrow,
A tilt of the head, but cannot see myself.

Though like each other, they are not like me.
But I can see in them, something of my father.
Uncles, home on leave during the war.   15

At three or four, I loved those straightbacked men
Towering above me, smiling and confident.
The whole world before them. Or so it seemed.

I look at my boys, slouched in armchairs
They have outgrown. See Tom in army uniform   20
And Finn in air force blue. Time is up.

Bearhugs. They lift me off my feet
And fifty years fall away. One son
After another, crushing the life into me.

GUIDELINES

Like the rest of McGough's poetry, 'Bearhugs' is a simple, straightforward account of a commonplace incident: a visit from two of his sons who no longer live with him, but with his first wife. 'Time is up' (line 21) suggests that the visit has to be of limited duration.

The visit is seen from the father's point of view. This, and all the other visits they make to him, are considered by him in two ways. Visits provide a means of assessing the boys, trying to discover what resemblances he can find between the two boys and other family members belonging to an earlier generation. They remind him, not of himself, but of his father and his uncles. This thought leads to a related one: the fine, upright stance of his uncles on leave from the front, and their disappointed hopes.

The visit has another significance for the father. It is, as he puts it, 'a reassurance of love unspoken' (line 9). The first three lines of the poem, along with the last three, show how this reassurance, so important to the father, is expressed. The repetition of 'Bearhugs' in these lines and in the title of the poem, suggests the urgent need felt by the father for confirmation of the love his sons have for him. Their vigorous expression of this love revives his spirit, and makes him feel young once more, as he relives the time when, as small children, they hugged him affectionately.

QUESTIONS

1 Does this poem help to explain why McGough has a wide appeal?
2 Comment on the language of the poem. What is its effect on you?
3 How does the poem make you feel about the father?
4 Why do you think the father needs reassurance? Does he get this from his sons?
5 Comment on the parallel between the sixth and seventh stanzas.
6 Discuss the significance of the contrast between 'crushing the life out of me' (line 3) and 'crushing the life into me' (line 24).

JOHN MONTAGUE

B. 1929

BIOGRAPHY

John Montague was born in Brooklyn, New York, on 28 February, 1929. His parents were Irish emigrants. During the war of Independence, his father James was an Irish volunteer whose activities included participation in ambushes and house-burning. He emigrated to New York in 1925. In Ireland, he had been unsuccessful in business ventures financed from the sale of his farm. He became a ticket collector in the New York subway. His wife and two young sons joined him later.

John left New York at the age of four with his mother and two brothers when his father could no longer support the family. Although his mother also returned to Tyrone, she took little or no part in his upbringing. He was reared by two aunts who lived in his father's home in Garvaghey and he grew up without knowing his father.

He was educated at Garvaghey Primary School and later at St Patrick's College Armagh. In 1946, he won a scholarship to University College Dublin. He later studied at Yale and Berkeley, two famous American Universities. One of his teachers at St Patrick's College was Sean O'Boyle, a leading authority on Ulster folksong and Irish poetry. O'Boyle gave him a love of the Gaelic tradition, which was to have a profound influence on his life and on his poetry.

Montague published his first collection of poems, *Forms of Exile*, in 1958. In the 1960s, he taught Anglo-Irish literature at UCD and in 1967 he issued *A Chosen Light*. In the late l960s he responded with enthusiasm to the Northern Ireland Civil Rights Movement and dedicated a collection of poems, *A New Siege*, to Bernadette Devlin, our of the leaders of the movement.

In 1972, he published *The Rough Field*, in which he explored Ulster and family history. Other important collections of his poetry include *A Slow Dance* (1975); *Poisoned Lands* (1977); *The Great Cloak* (1975); *Selected Poems* (1982) and *The Dead Kingdom* (1984). *A Slow Dance* is particularly interesting for its treatment of the Northern Ireland conflict. In one of the poems in that collection, 'Falls Funeral', there is a chillingly realistic account of the burial of a murdered Catholic child. In another, 'Northern Express', Montague shows how the horrors of the struggle can affect ordinary people. Some of the poems in *The Dead Kingdom* deal with his father's lonely life in Brooklyn.

Montague has held a wide variety of positions throughout his adult life. He has been a film-critic, a proof-reader, an editor, a university lecturer and a writer-in-residence at many American universities. In 1998 he was appointed to The Ireland Chair of Poetry, which is supported by the Ireland Fund. Since the l970s, he has been based in Cork, lecturing at University College there and running poetry workshops. He was the first significant twentieth-century poet writing from a Northern Irish Catholic background. He established a tradition which has been followed by others from a similar background, including Seamus Heaney.

SOCIAL AND CULTURAL CONTEXT

Montague's poetry reflects his lifelong interest in the history, mythology and landscape of his ancestral home in Co. Tyrone. It was natural for a poet born in exile to display more than an ordinary interest in the world in which his father and mother grew up, as well as in their neighbours and relatives. In one of his most distinguished early poems, 'Like Dolmens Round My Childhood, The Old People', he combines reference to the ancient landscape of Tyrone and its prehistoric burial customs with an exploration of the mysterious old characters who fired his imagination during his childhood in Tyrone. In this poem, the people and their way of life are of much greater interest to the poet than are the relics of ancient times. Montague does, however, suggest an intimate link between past and present. His old and eccentric neighbours have inherited ancient customs from their primitive past. This makes it possible for him to feel that the past still lives through the lives of Jamie Mac Crystal, Maggie Owens, the Nialls and Wild Billy Eagleson:

Ancient Ireland, indeed! I was reared by her bedside,
The rune and the chant, evil eye and averted head,
Fomorian fierceness of family and local fend.

In 'The Wild Dog Rose', Montague might have turned the Cailleach, the terrible woman who terrified him when he was a child, into a creature of myth. Instead, he discovers in her a creature in the grip of loneliness and fear.

Many of Montague's poems are based on the poet's own family history and are strongly autobiographical. Memories of his father are often his major themes. In 'The Cage', for example, he recalls his father's unhappy life in New York, trying to preserve his identity as 'a traditional Irishman by drinking neat whiskey'. His father's ultimately successful struggle with his addiction to alcohol made Montague proud. After his father's death, he paid envious tribute to his freedom from addiction for fifteen years, remarking that 'if you're an alcoholic that's quite heroic'. A second quality he admired in his father was that he was 'an intensely believing Catholic'. Montague remembered thinking his 'poor old battered father quite noble' when he saw him laid out in a Franciscan habit. He believed that the power of his religious faith 'enabled him to surmount in himself a life which, he said himself, he had frittered away'. In 'The Locket', the poet's relationship with his mother is affectionately explored. Montague constructs his poem out of the miserable life endured by his mother, partly the result of his father's inability to support a wife and family, and partly the result of adverse circumstances: she had arrived at her husband's doorstep just in time for The Great Depression of 1929.

Montague does not focus exclusively on the limited set of themes suggested in the poems mentioned above: family life in New York, family relationships and Tyrone relationships. 'A Welcoming Party' suggests a broader vision of the world. Here, Montague ironically explores the detachment of Irish children from the realities of total war, his own 'parochial brand of innocence' in the face of a film showing a concentration camp. In this poem, an individual experience takes on a universal meaning.

THE CAGE

My father, the least happy
man I have known. His face
retained the pallor
of those who work underground:
the lost years in Brooklyn   5
listening to a subway
shudder the earth.

But a traditional Irishman
who (released from his grille
in the Clark St I.R.T.)   10
drank neat whiskey until
he reached the only element
he felt at home in
any longer: brute oblivion.

And yet picked himself   15
up, most mornings,
to march down the street
extending his smile
to all sides of the good
(non-negro) neighbourhood   20
belled by St. Teresa's church.

When he came back
we walked together
across fields of Garvaghey
to see hawthorn on the summer   25
hedges, as though
he had never left;
a bend on the road

which still sheltered
primroses. But we
did not smile in   30
the shared complicity
of a dream, for when
weary Odysseus returns
Telemachus must leave.   35

Often as I descend
into subway or underground
I see his bald head behind
the bars of the small booth;
the mark of an old car   40
accident beating on his
ghostly forehead.

GLOSSARY

   3 *pallor*: an unnatural paleness

   5 *Brooklyn*: a borough of New York. Many Irish emigrants lived there

   6 *subway*: New York underground rail system

   7 *shudder*: to shake violently

   9 *grille*: a metal screen with bars. His duties as a subway ticket collector meant
      that the poet's father had to work behind a grille. Here it refers to the subway
      ticket office where the poet's father worked

  10 *the Clark St I.R.T.*: a New York subway station

  11 *neat whiskey*: undiluted whiskey

  12 *the only element*: the only condition

  14 *oblivion*: forgetfulness

  18 *extending*: reaching out with

19–21 *to all sides … … church*: the speaker's father was happy to smile at the white
      inhabitants of the white neighbourhood, served by the local Catholic Church

  22 *came back*: returned to Ireland

  24 *Garvaghey*: the birthplace of the poet's father, who returned to Ireland in 1952,
      nineteen years after John had been sent back

29–32 *But we …of a dream*: we did not share the same dreams, hopes or ambitions

  31 *complicity*: involvement

32–34 *for when … must leave*: Odysseus, also called Ulysses, is the hero of Homer's Epic
poem, *The Odyssey*. His adventures on land and on sea last twenty years.
Telemachus is the son of Odysseus. In Homer's poem, Telemachus and his mother
Penelope wait at their home in Ithaca for the return of Odysseus. When Odysseus
comes home, Telemachus leaves Ithaca. There are obvious parallels between this
story and that of the Montague family. The most striking one is that the younger
Montague left for New York as soon as his father came back from there

39 *booth*: a small enclosed structure

GUIDELINES

The poem is about Montague's father, James. It is also about the father-son
relationship, and about the effects of exile and return on a man described in
Stanza Two as 'a traditional Irishman'. Montague's father, 'the least happy /
man I have known', according to the poet, had every reason to be unhappy. His
militant patriotism induced him to flee to New York. His failure to earn an
adequate living and his fondness for drink alienated his wife for whom, as we
learn in 'The Locket', all his songs 'couldn't sweeten the lack of money'.

Abandoned by his wife and family in the early 1930s, he was obliged to live
alone in New York until his retirement from a menial job in 1952, when he
returned to Ireland to live out the last seven years of his life in Omagh, Co Tyrone.

The first three stanzas of the poem provide a concise account of James
Montague's life as an Irish emigrant in New York. It is significant that Montague
describes his father's time in New York as 'the lost years'. The suggestion here is
that exile from the place of his ancestors deprives his life of its essential meaning
and robs him of his identity. The title of the poem is a metaphor for James
Montague's plight. He spends his working life underground in a subway ticket
office, a kind of miniature prison in which he must dispense tickets through the
bars of a grille. He is pale-faced from lack of fresh air, his ears assaulted by the
noise of the subway trains as they 'shudder the earth'. His pale colour suggests
death, which is also brought to mind by the image of the underground. This
word invokes thoughts of Hades, the home of the dead in Greek mythology.

What he has lost through exile is suggested in Stanzas Four and Five: the
fields of his native Garvaghey, 'hawthorn on the summer / hedges' and primroses
sheltered by a bend in the road. Life in the infernal underground cage can be
relieved only in the 'brute oblivion' of drunkenness, another kind of imprisonment. The contrast between these forms of physical and mental captivity and
the freedom of the open fields of Garvaghey is central to the meaning of the

poem. James Montague's underground life behind the grille of the Clark Street subway station becomes a metaphor for his life as an exile who cannot feel at home in New York and who tries to find a substitute home in a state of forgetfulness induced by neat whiskey. The cage suggests another kind of double life. He is visible through its bars and at the same time cut off from a world to which he does not fully belong.

Stanzas Four and Five refer to James Montague's return from America in 1952, when father and son could spend time together in Garvaghey. The end of the father's exile does not, however, mark the beginning of a happy relationship between father and son. They 'did not smile in / the shared complicity / of a dream'. When James Montague, like the weary Odysseus of Homer's ancient epic, comes home, his son, like Telemachus, son of Odysseus, must himself go into exile. His place of exile is New York, the one originally chosen by his father.

The final stanza of the poem is based on the notion that the father is a double for his son, just as the son is a double for him. To reinforce this point, Montague uses an image of his dead father behind the bars of a subway booth:

> the mark of an old car
> accident beating on his
> ghostly forehead.

Elsewhere in his work, Montague is at pains to stress the physical resemblance between his father and himself, in particular the detail of a facial scar common to both as a means of suggesting that he sees his father as an image of himself.

QUESTIONS

1 Why do you think the poet chose 'The Cage' as the title of this poem? Explore the ideas associated with the image of the cage throughout the poem.

2 How would you describe the poet's attitude to his father? Refer to words or phrases in the poem.

3 Explain the reference to 'the lost years in Brooklyn'.

4 Why did the poet's father seek comfort in 'brute oblivion'?

5 The poet tells us that his father extended his smile 'to all sides of the good / (non-negro) neighbourhood'. Explain this reference.

6 How is the idea of imprisonment suggested in Stanza Two of the poem?

7 In Stanza Five, we are told that father and son did not smile in 'the shared complicity / of a dream'. Why do you think this was so? What was the dream?

8 Comment on the reference to Odysseus and Telemachus in Stanza Five.

9 Say what you like or dislike about this poem.

10 On the evidence of the poem, does the father's life seem to have served any purpose?

11 The poem features some significant examples of contrast. Discuss some of these, for example, the contrast between Brooklyn and Garvaghey.

12 What do the images in the final stanza of the poem suggest to you ('I descend'; 'underground'; 'bars'; 'ghostly forehead')?

LIKE DOLMENS ROUND MY CHILDHOOD, THE OLD PEOPLE

Like dolmens round my childhood, the old people.

Jamie MacCrystal sang to himself,
A broken song without tune, without words;
He tipped me a penny every pension day,
Fed kindly crusts to winter birds   5
When he died, his cottage was robbed,
Mattress and money box torn and searched.
Only the corpse they didn't disturb.

Maggie Owens was surrounded by animals,
A mongrel bitch and shivering pups,   10
Even in her bedroom a she-goat cried.
She was a well of gossip defiled,
Fanged chronicler of a whole countryside:
Reputed a witch, all I could find
Was her lonely need to deride.   15

The Nialls lived along a mountain lane
Where heather bells bloomed, clumps of foxglove.
All were blind, with Blind Pension and Wireless,
Dead eyes serpent-flicked as one entered
To shelter from a downpour of mountain rain.
Crickets chirped under the rocking hearthstone   20
Until the muddy sun shone out again.

Mary Moore lived in a crumbling gatehouse,
Famous as Pisa for its leaning gable.
Bag-apron and boots, she tramped the fields
Driving lean cattle from a miry stable.   25
A by-word for fierceness, she fell asleep
Over love stories, Red Star and Red Circle,
Dreamed of gypsy love rites, by firelight sealed.

Wile Billy Eagleson married a Catholic servant girl   30
When all his Loyal family passed on:
We danced round him shouting 'To Hell with King Billy,'
And dodged from the arc of his flailing blackthorn.
Forsaken by both creeds, he showed little concern
Until the Orange drums banged past in the summer   35
And bowler and sash aggressively shone.

Curate and doctor trudged to attend them,
Through knee-deep snow, through summer heat,
From main road to lane to broken path,
Gulping the mountain air with painful breath.   40
Sometimes they were found by neighbours,
Silent keepers of a smokeless hearth,
Suddenly cast in the mould of death.

Ancient Ireland, indeed! I was reared by her bedside,
The rune and the chant, evil eye and averted head,   45
Fomorian fierceness of family and local feud.
Gaunt figures of fear and of friendliness,
For years they trespassed on my dreams,
Until once, in a standing circle of stones,
I felt their shadows pass   50

Into that dark permanence of ancient forms.

GLOSSARY

1 *dolmens*: prehistoric monuments usually consisting of several great stone slabs set edgewise in the earth to support a flat stone, which served as a roof. Dolmens were designed as burial structures

12 *She was …defiled*: she told foul stories about her neighbours

13 *Fanged chronicler*: teller of bitter, biting stories

14 *Reputed a witch*: having the reputation of being a witch

15 *Was her lonely need to deride*: her loneliness caused her to mock other people

18 *All were blind … Wireless*: those who were blind were entitled to a pension and a radio from the social welfare services

23 *gatehouse*: a house occupied by the caretaker of a larger house

24 *Pisa*: a reference to the leaning tower in that city

25 *miry*: muddy

27 *Red Star and Red Circle*: magazines featuring love stories

31 *Loyal family*: a family which supported the connection between Northern Ireland and the United Kingdom

32 *King Billy*: King William of Orange, a Protestant hero

34 *Forsaken by both creeds*: abandoned by members of both religions

35 *Until the Orange drums … summer*: until the arrival of the Orange Order marching season

36 *bowler and sash*: these are worn by members of the Orange Order during their marches

37 *Curate*: Catholic priest

45 *rune and chant*: a rune was a song or set of words believed to have magic properties. The chant has a similar meaning

46 *evil eye and averted head*: people who had the evil eye were believed to have the power to bring disaster on those they looked at. To avoid this, people turned away or averted their heads

47 *Fomorian*: the Fomorians were a savage tribe of ancient settlers in Ireland

47 *feud*: long-standing dispute often involving several generations of the same families

47 *Gaunt*: thin

48 *trespassed on my dreams*: invaded my dreams

49 *standing circle of stones*: in ancient Ireland, stone circles were associated with the worship of the sun

50–51 *I felt their shadows pass … forms*: the ancient forms that haunted him have passed away forever

GUIDELINES

This poem deals with some of the more unusual people who inhabited the world of Montague's childhood. Like many of Montague's poems, this one features fully human individuals, scarred by misery and suffering but also possessing faith and enjoying life. The main characters in the poem are isolated, lonely people. For the young Montague, their main significance was that they haunted his childhood dreams, conjuring up sinister and grotesque images associated with ancient pagan customs. In early adult life, when childhood gave way to manhood, the dark dreams no longer troubled him. He traces his liberation from their fearful grip to a single experience. Standing as a young man in a circle of stones, he feels the terrible shadow cast by the old people pass away and the dreams, which have troubled him are transformed into myth, 'that dark permanence of ancient forms'.

The dolmens mentioned in the title and in the first line of the poem have a symbolic meaning. By imagining the old people as dolmens, the poet is suggesting why Jamie Mac Crystal, Maggie Owens and the others dominated his life and troubled even his dreams. He was imprisoned by their influence in much the same way as the body of an ancient inhabitant of Ireland was buried beneath a dolmen. There is a further dimension to the comparison between dolmens and old people. To the poet's eye, the human figures are scattered around the landscape like figures of stone.

The poem, however, is one of liberation as well as of imprisonment. This becomes clear in the last stanza. Just as the dolmens represent the child's captivity, the standing circle of stones is associated with his release from the fearful dreams inspired by the old people. The last stanza tells us that his escape from the shadow cast on his young life by his elderly neighbours coincides with his entry into manhood. The act of making the old people present in his poetry serves a purpose similar to exorcism. They become in the end external to his mind and find their permanence in stone.

To the child's imagination all the characters of the poem are forbidding, abnormal and sometimes grotesque. Jamie Mac Crystal's song without tune and without words is sung to himself. Maggie Owens is thought to be a witch and keeps a she-goat in her bedroom. The Nialls are all blind. Mary Moore is remarkable for her fierceness, while Billy Eagleson is wild and wields a flailing blackthorn. These primitive people carry on some of the pagan traditions of ancient Ireland. There is, however, more to them than this. They may be 'Gaunt figures of fear', but as the last stanza admits they also appeal to the poet's imagination as figures of friendliness. In spite of their forbidding appearance the poet is able to feel sympathy for them and to understand the motives behind their behaviour. Jamie Mac Crystal is a poor man but still gives a penny to the young Montague every pension day and feeds hungry winter birds. Maggie Owens is a notorious gossip but the poet feels able to explain this by suggesting that frustration and loneliness cause her to speak ill of her neighbours. She has suffered much in her isolation.

QUESTIONS

1 In the title and in the first line, the poet relates the old people to dolmens. What is the significance of this relationship?

2 The old people mentioned in the poem have a few things in common. Mention as many of these as you can.

3 What is the poet's attitude to the people he is describing. Explain your answer by referring to words or phrases from the poem.

4 Which of the people do you think had a) the happiest life, and b) the saddest life. Refer to the poem for examples.

5 Maggie Owens is not the woman she seems. Explain this idea.

6 The old people are described as 'Silent keepers of a smokeless hearth / Suddenly cast in the mould of death'. What does this mean? Has 'mould' more than one meaning in this context?

7 Is the poem sad or comic or both? Explain.

8 Choose your favourite character from the poem. Give reasons for your choice.

9 Why is Billy Eagleson 'forsaken by both creeds'? What effect do the 'Orange drums' have on his attitudes?

10 What does the poet mean when he claims that he was reared by the bedside of 'Ancient Ireland'? Develop your answer by referring to the poem.

11 Why do you think the poet describes his neighbours as 'Gaunt figures of fear and friendliness'?

12 How did the old people trespass on the poet's dreams? How did he free himself from the influence of these dreams?

PAUL MULDOON

B. 1951

BIOGRAPHY

Paul Muldoon was born in Portadown, Co. Armagh on 20 June, 1951. His mother was a teacher, his father a labourer and market gardener. He was educated at St Patrick's College, Armagh, and at the Queen's University, Belfast, where the poet Seamus Heaney was his tutor. Muldoon's first collection of poems, *New Weather*, was published in 1973 while he was 22 and still at university.

Muldoon has worked as a radio and television producer for BBC Northern Ireland and he has held writing fellowships at various universities including Cambridge University, Columbia University (New York) and the University of California at Berkeley. Since 1990 he has been a Professor of the Humanities and Creative Writing at Princeton University.

Muldoon has received many awards for his poetry, including the Sir Geoffrey Faber Memorial Award in 1991, the T. S. Eliot Memorial Prize in 1994 for his collection *The Annals of Chile* and the American Academy of Arts and Letters Award for Literature in 1996. In May 1999 he was appointed Professor of Poetry at Oxford University. His *New Selected Poems 1968–1994,* published in 1996, won the prestigious *Irish Times* Irish Literature Prize for Poetry in 1997. He has edited a number of poetry anthologies, among them *The Faber Book of Contemporary Irish Poetry* (1986), and he has also written a play for television, *Monkeys* (1989). His collection *Moy Sand and Gravel* (2002) was awarded the Pulitzer Prize in 2003.

He lives in the USA with his novelist wife Jean Hanff Korelitz and their daughter.

ANSEO

When the Master was calling the roll
At the primary school in Collegelands,
You were meant to call back *Anseo*
And raise your hand
As your name occurred.   5
Anseo, meaning here, here and now,
All present and correct,
Was the first word of Irish I spoke.
The last name on the ledger
Belonged to Joseph Mary Plunkett Ward   10
And was followed, as often as not,
By silence, knowing looks,
A nod and a wink, the Master's droll
'And where's our little Ward-of-court?'

I remember the first time he came back   15
The Master had sent him out
Along the hedges
To weigh up for himself and cut
A stick with which he would be beaten.
After a while, nothing was spoken;   20
He would arrive as a matter of course
With an ash-plant, a salley-rod.
Or finally, the hazel-wand
He had whittled down to a whip-lash,
Its twist of red and yellow lacquers   25
Sanded and polished,
And altogether so delicately wrought
That he had engraved his initials on it.

I last met Joseph Mary Plunkett Ward
In a pub just over the Irish border.   30
He was living in the open,
In a secret camp
On the other side of the mountain.
He was fighting for Ireland,
Making things happen.   35
And he told me, Joe Ward,
Of how he had risen through the ranks
To Quartermaster, Commandant:
How every morning at parade
His volunteers would call back *Anseo*   40
And raise their hands
As their names occurred.

GLOSSARY

title *Anseo*: the Irish word for 'present', in answer to a roll call

2 *Collegelands*: an area in Co. Armagh near where the poet was brought up

9 *ledger*: register, roll

10 *Joseph Mary Plunkett Ward*: the boy was clearly called after Joseph Mary Plunkett, executed after the Rising of 1916

13 *droll*: amusing

14 *Ward-of-court*: a play on the phrase 'ward of court', to be in the care of the courts

22 *salley-rod*: a type of stick cut from the salley tree

24 *whittled down to a whip-lash*: pared down until it became like a whip

25 *lacquers*: varnishes

27 *wrought*: made

38 *Quartermaster*: a staff officer in the army (here, the IRA)

GUIDELINES

'Anseo' is from the volume *Why Brownlee Left* (1980). It was written when the Northern Ireland conflict, known as 'The Troubles', seemed to have no solution.

Stanza One: Irish children have often used the Irish word 'Anseo', meaning 'present', during roll call at school, as the speaker and his classmates did at primary school in Collegelands, Co. Armagh. One of the boys in the class, Joseph Mary Plunkett Ward, was often absent, a fact remarked on sarcastically by the teacher.

The boy's name is significant in the context of Irish history (see annotations above). As the poem is set in Northern Ireland it suggests that his parents' political views were those of the Irish Catholic Nationalists. The reasons why he was absent from school are not explained. Nor are we given any explanation why the 'Master' (schoolteacher) reacted as he did, with his rather feeble pun on the boy's last name.

Stanza Two: The speaker remembers how the teacher would send Joseph Mary Plunkett Ward out to cut a stick with which he would beat him. He describes in an unemotional way how the boy became so used to being beaten that he would arrive at school with the stick already cut. The sticks are described almost as if they were beautiful objects, 'Sanded and polished'. Even the boy himself seems immune to being punished. He has gone so far as to carve his own initials on the stick.

When you read these lines it is easy to gloss over the fact that corporal punishment was an accepted part of school life. Not only that, but to our modern minds it seems incredible that a child would be asked to prepare his own instrument of punishment, as he was. The speaker does not make any comment, underlining perhaps the fact that generations of children did not question the treatment they sometimes got at school.

Stanza Three: These lines suggest that his treatment at school had a profound effect on Joe Ward's later career. We see him as an adult, now a member of the Irish Republican Army, involved in the Northern Ireland conflict known as 'The Troubles'. It is clear that he is now in a position of power over others, as the teacher had once been over him. Ironically, he calls the roll in exactly the same way as the master had in school, so that the volunteers must answer 'Anseo'.

THE THEME OF THE POEM

The poet/speaker makes no direct comment on Joe Ward (as he is now known) or his situation. The connection is clear, though, between the boy's treatment at school and his later life of violence. His experience of being brutalised by the schoolteacher has made him insensitive to the pain of others or the damage his actions may cause. Perhaps this is one of the themes of the poem: what happens to us in childhood affects the way we live later on and what we do. Ironically, though, Joe Ward seems unaware of this. Is this the worst irony of all?

QUESTIONS

1 What impression of primary school life does this poem give us?

2 What aspect of the story do you find most disturbing? Give reasons for your view.

3 Why do you think the poet describes the hazel-wand in such detail in the second stanza?

4 Do you think there is a connection between Joe Ward's early experiences at school and his activities in the IRA? Or is there a more complex reason for his activities? Might it have any connection with his personal circumstances, including the name given to him by his parents? Look again at the first stanza.

5 Which of these words would come closest to describing the tone of the poem, in your opinion: angry, disappointed, bitter, disgusted, detached? Refer to the poem in support of your views.

6 What, in your opinion, is the main point the poem makes? Do you agree with it?

7 Imagine you are one of Joe Ward's 'Volunteers'. Write a short account of the life you lead and say what you think of your leader.

RICHARD MURPHY

B. 1927

BIOGRAPHY

Richard Murphy was born in Galway. His father, Sir William Lindsay Murphy, was in the British Colonial Service, and Murphy spent his childhood in Ceylon and the Bahamas. He attended Oxford and the Sorbonne in Paris. He lived and worked in Crete before returning to Ireland in the early 1960s. He set up home on Inisbofin, making his living from an old sailing boat, which he restored. His 1963 collection, *Sailing to an Island*, won wide acclaim.

In 1985, Murphy's book, *The Price of Stone*, charted his colourful life through the houses and buildings he'd known. The book ranged over his colonial childhood, his English education and his life on a small island. His 1968 book on the Battle of Aughrim is of interest for many reasons, not least because his ancestors fought on both sides.

Murphy's work has always been highly regarded both at home and abroad. Among his most famous literary friends were the poets Ted Hughes and Sylvia Plath. Their visit to him in September 1962, a short time before Plath's death, has received much attention from her biographers.

Richard Murphy now divides his time between Dublin and Durban in South Africa. His *Collected Poems* was published in 2000.

THE READING LESSON

Fourteen years old, learning the alphabet,
He finds letters harder to catch than hares
Without a greyhound. Can't I give him a dog
To track them down, or put them in a cage?
He's caught in a trap, until I let him go,   5
Pinioned by 'Don't you want to learn to read?'
'I'll be the same man whatever I do.'

He looks at a page as a mule balks at a gap
From which a goat may hobble out and bleat.
His eyes jink from a sentence like flushed snipe   10
Escaping shot. A sharp word, and he'll mooch
Back to his piebald mare and bantam cock.
Our purpose is as tricky to retrieve
As mercury from a smashed thermometer.

'I'll not read any more.' Should I give up?   15
His hands, long-fingered as a Celtic scribe's,
Will grow callous, gathering sticks or scrap;
Exploring pockets of the horny drunk
Loiterers at the fairs, giving them lice.
A neighbour chuckles. 'You can never tame   20
The wild duck: when his wings grow, he'll fly off.'

If books resembled roads, he'd quickly read:
But they're small farms to him, fenced by the page,
Ploughed into lines, with letters drilled like oats:
A field of tasks he'll always be outside.   25
If words were bank notes, he would filch a wad;
If they were pheasants, they'd be in his pot
For breakfast, or if wrens he'd make them king.

GLOSSARY

8 *balks*: hesitates, refuses to go on

10 *jink*: dodge or move away

11 *mooch*: move in a half-hearted way

16 *scribe*: a person, usually a monk, who made copies of books. The Book of Kells was made by scribes

16–17 *a Celtic scribe's…sticks or scraps*: a remarkable feature of the poem is the way in which sounds are repeated and echoed across lines and stanzas, as in the tradition of poetry written in Irish

17 *callous*: hardened and thick-skinned

26 *filch*: steal, pilfer

GUIDELINES

The speaker of the poem describes giving a reading lesson to a 14 year-old boy. The poem uses a series of colourful images to suggest the boy's difficulty in mastering letters and words. The images are drawn from the boy's world.

The first line establishes the dramatic situation. The lesson is for a boy, who is almost a man in the Traveller culture to which he belongs, but who has not yet learned to read. The first line also establishes the style of the poem. It is written in lines of ten syllables, the traditional line length for poets writing in English, going back to the time of Shakespeare. However, the poem imitates some of the sound patterns of poetry written in Irish, thereby combining both an Irish and an English tradition of poetry.

In lines 2 and 3, the narrator introduces the first of many comparisons that describe what the boy cannot do by drawing attention to the things he can do. The boy feels trapped in the reading lesson. However, for the teacher, reading is a form of freedom. The final line of the first stanza, 'I'll be the same man whatever I do', illustrates the boy's pride, defiance and, perhaps, his vulnerability.

In the second stanza the comparison of the boy to a mule suggests the boy's awkward, stubborn, possibly belligerent attitude to the task of learning to read. The narrator continues to describe the boy's reaction to reading with images taken from the boy's world in which animals play a large part.

The reference to the scribe in Stanza Three is a reminder that the Travellers are inheritors of the Celtic tradition. Perhaps it suggests that the loss of reading and writing is a loss of the boy's birthright? The comment of the neighbour, 'You can never tame / The wild duck: when his wings grow, he'll fly off,' raises the question of whether the teacher is trying to turn the boy into something that he is not. However, the motivation of the teacher can be interpreted as a desire to save the boy from the rough, dirty life that lies ahead of him.

There is a change of tone in the final stanza. The teacher seems to have abandoned his or her efforts to teach the boy. The stanza is composed of a series of 'If only' statements which express regret at the failure to help the boy to read while speaking affectionately of him. The final image concludes the poem on a note of celebration and flight.

QUESTIONS

1 In the first stanza the speaker compares the boy's difficulty in reading to catching hares without a greyhound. In the context of the poem, is this a good image?

2 What, do you think, is the tone of the boy's remark, 'I'll be the same man whatever I do.' What does this line reveal to us about the boy?

3 What comparisons (similes) are used in Stanza Two to describe the way the boy looks at the page? What do they tell us about the boy?

4 a) What makes the job of teaching the boy so 'tricky'?
b) What is the neighbour's attitude to the reading lesson (lines 20–21)?

5 What future does the speaker foresee for the boy (lines 16–19)?

6 'A field of tasks he'll always be outside' (line 25). The last stanza tells us much about the boy's world and way of life. Write a short piece describing this life, incorporating all the information given in the stanza.

7 Select three words, phrases or images that you like most in the poem. Explain your choice.

8 Take a stanza and count the number of syllables in each line. Examine the rhymes/half rhymes used by the poet. Look at any two lines and comment on the sounds in the lines and their effect.

9 'Should I give up?' (line 15). By the end of the poem, do you think the teacher has given up? Explain your answer.

10 It has been said that in his poetry Richard Murphy often celebrates people who are outsiders. Is the boy in this poem an outsider? Explain your answer.

SHARON OLDS

B. 1942

BIOGRAPHY

Sharon Olds was born in 1942 in San Francisco. She was educated at Stanford University and Columbia University. Her first book of poems, *Satan Says* (1980), received the San Francisco Poetry Center Award, while her second book, *The Dead and the Living* (1983) was the winner of the National Book Critics' Circle Award. Her other poetry collections include *The Gold Cell*, *The Father*, *The Wellspring* and *Blood, Tin, Straw*.

Sharon Olds has been writer-in-residence at a number of academic institutions in the USA. In recent years she has taught poetry workshops in the Graduate Program in Creative Writing at New York University and in the NYU workshop at Goldwater Hospital for the severely disabled in New York. She was appointed New York State Poet for 1998–2000.

LOOKING AT THEM ASLEEP

When I come home late at night and go in to kiss the children,
I see my girl with her arm curled around her head,
her face deep in unconsciousness—so
deeply centered she is in her dark self,
her mouth slightly puffed like one sated but   5
slightly pouted like one who hasn't had enough,
her eyes so closed you would think they have rolled the
iris around to face the back of her head,
the eyeball marble-naked under that
thick satisfied desiring lid,   10
she lies on her back in abandon and sealed completion,
and the son in his room, oh the son he is sideways in his bed,
one knee up as if he is climbing
sharp stairs up into the night,
and under his thin quivering eyelids you   15
know his eyes are wide open and
staring and glazed, the blue in them so
anxious and crystally in all this darkness, and his
mouth is open, he is breathing hard from the climb
and panting a bit, his brow is crumpled   20
and pale, his long fingers curved,
his hand open, and in the center of each hand
the dry dirty boyish palm
resting like a cookie. I look at him in his
quest, the thin muscles of his arms   25
passionate and tense, I look at her with her
face like the face of a snake who has swallowed a deer,
content, content—and I know if I wake her she'll
smile and turn her face toward me though
half asleep and open her eyes and I   30
know if I wake him he'll jerk and say Don't and sit
up and stare about him in blue
unrecognition, oh my Lord how I
know these two. When love comes to me and says
What do you know, I say This girl, this boy.   35

5 *sated*: fully satisfied

6 *pouted*: pushed forward in an attitude of sulkiness. Can also indicate seductiveness. Some of the language used to describe the girl has erotic connotations

8 *iris*: the round, coloured part of the eye

15 *quivering eyelids*: trembling. The movement of the eyelids is said to indicate the state of dreaming

20 *crumpled*: wrinkled

25 *quest*: an adventure, a journey, a search, especially that of a knight

GUIDELINES

In the poem the speaker describes her sleeping children and the feelings which she experiences as she looks at them asleep. Her daughter's sleep is more peaceful than her son's. She sleeps in a way that suggests a deep contentment. In her daughter's mouth and lips the speaker sees something of the girl's personality – someone who is satisfied even as she desires a little more.

In comparison to his sister, the boy's sleep is agitated. The speaker imagines him involved in some dream activity, a quest that involves physical effort and exertion. In his furrowed brow she reads tension and anxiety.

The speaker tells us that she knows how each of her children would react if she woke them. Her girl would smile at her but her boy would look at her without recognition, still involved in the world of his sleeping. And looking at her sleeping children, the speaker is overcome with a sense of her love for them and her knowledge of them.

The poem is rich in sounds and sound echoes and composed in carefully-crafted phrases. The language used to describe the girl's sleeping suggests sleep as the completion or end of activity ('sated', 'satisfied', 'sealed'), while the language used to describe the boy's sleep suggests endless activity ('climbing', 'quivering', 'panting').

There is an interesting tension in the poem between the idea of a parent's knowledge of his/her children and the dream world of these children to which the parent has no access. Examine, for example, the language used to describe the girl's sleep. She is 'deep in unconsciousness'; she is 'deeply centered in her dark self'. Her eyes are 'so closed' that the speaker imagines the iris rolled around to the back of the head. As the speaker looks at the girl she lies in 'sealed completion'. What these phrases suggest is the extent to which the child is in another place, far from the consciousness of the parent who observes her, so the claim to knowledge, made at the end of the poem, may be less strong than a claim to love.

QUESTIONS

1 The poem has no rhyme scheme and is written in lines of irregular length. What, in your opinion, are the poetic qualities it possesses?

2 '… so / deeply centered she is in her dark self …'. What do you think is the meaning of this line? Is the dark self something which can be known by others?

3 The speaker refers to 'my girl' and 'the son'. Is this a significant difference? Is it indicative a difference in the speaker's attitude to her daughter and to her son elsewhere in the poem?

4 Where, do you think, is the language of the poem most affectionate in relation to the children?

5 Describe difference between the girl's sleep and the boy's sleep. In the case of each, select two phrases that you think are particularly effective in describing their manner of sleep.

6 'On the evidence of this poem, the girl will lead a happier life than the boy.' Give your view of this statement.

7 What age do you think the children are in the poem? If you were one of the children who inspired the poem, how would you react to being described in this way? Explain your answer.

8 'The poem is a statement of a parent's love and loyalty.'
'The poem is an exercise in betrayal and exploitation.'
Give your view of these contrasting assessments of the poem.

9 'The speaker of the poem may love her children but the poem demonstrates that however much we love someone they remain a mystery to us.' Give your response to this statement.

10 Sharon Olds has said she wants to be accurate about thoughts and feelings in her poetry. In your opinion does she succeed in 'Looking at Them Asleep'?

11 Family life, parenthood, death and erotic love are the subjects of Sharon Olds' poetry. Do you think 'Looking at Them Asleep' contains elements of all four?

SYLVIA PLATH

1932–1963

BIOGRAPHY

Sylvia Plath was born in a seaside suburb of Boston in 1932. Both her parents, Otto Plath and Aurelia Schober, were academics and had German ancestry. They believed in the virtues of hard work and were committed to education. Sylvia was a bright, intelligent child and won many school prizes and awards.

When Sylvia was eight, her father fell ill. Convinced that he had cancer, he refused to attend a doctor. When, eventually, a diagnosis was confirmed, he had to undergo an operation to amputate his leg. He died shortly afterwards. When Sylvia learned of his death, she declared, 'I'll never speak to God again'. Anxious to spare Sylvia and her younger brother Warren any unnecessary upset, their mother did not bring them to the funeral. Her father's death haunted Sylvia for the remainder of her life.

Otto Plath's death left the family in difficult financial circumstances. Aurelia Plath took up a full-time teaching job to support her children and Sylvia's grandparents moved in with the family in a house in the prosperous suburb of Wellesley. Later Sylvia wrote that the move to Wellesley marked the end of her idyllic childhood by the sea.

All through High School, Plath published poems and stories in local and national newspapers and in her school magazine. In her final year at school,

Seventeen, a national teen magazine, published her short story 'And Summer Will Not Come Again'. It was an important landmark in the young writer's life.

In 1951, Plath entered Smith College, an exclusive women's college in Massachusetts, with the help of two scholarships. Plath's first two years at Smith went well. Her talent and intelligence were nurtured by the teaching staff, her grades were excellent and she continued to have her work published. During her second year at Smith, she was awarded a fiction prize by *Mademoiselle*, a fashionable, upmarket magazine for young women. During this period she dated Dick Norton, a childhood friend from Wellesley who came from a wealthy background.

Despite these successes, academic, personal and social, Plath was deeply insecure about herself. The beginning of her third year in college saw her beset by many doubts and uncertainties. A four-week guest editorship at *Mademoiselle* in New York did little to improve matters. Failure to secure a place on a summer course run by Frank O'Connor at Harvard in 1953 caused a crisis, and she was sent for psychiatric treatment. A poorly supervised and administered series of electric shock treatments worsened her condition and she made an attempt to take her own life. She was missing for three days, unconscious in a narrow space under the family home. She recovered her health over a period of six months with the help of a sympathetic psychiatrist.

Smith College offered her a scholarship to allow her to finish her degree, and she returned to the college in spring 1954, graduating with distinction. By now she had acquired a growing reputation as a writer.

More success came her way in the form of a prestigious Fulbright scholarship to study at Cambridge University. She entered Newnham College in October 1955. It was in Cambridge that Sylvia Plath met the poet Ted Hughes. After a whirlwind romance, the couple married on Bloomsday, June 16, 1956. Plath returned to Cambridge to complete her studies in Autumn 1956, continuing all the while to write. At the same time she helped Hughes organise and send out his work. ('Black Rook in Rainy Weather' was written in this period.) The couple moved to America in summer 1957, and Plath taught for a year at Smith. She found the job taxing and considered herself to be a poor teacher. While Hughes continued to enjoy publishing success, Plath found it impossible to find time to devote to her writing in the way that she longed. At the end of the academic year in summer 1958, Plath resigned her teaching position at Smith, against her mother's wishes, and the couple rented a small apartment in Boston. The year was not without its difficulties. Plath suffered from writer's block and depression. 'The Times Are Tidy' was one of the few poems she completed. She was worried by financial concerns and tried to supplement their income by taking part-time secretarial work. By summer 1959, things had improved. Hughes continued to write and publish and Plath, too, completed both poems and short stories. The couple then decided to return to England. Before they left America, they spent two months at a writer's colony in New York State. Relieved of domestic duties, Plath wrote freely and finished a number of the poems that are included in *The Colossus*, the only collection published during her lifetime.

Frieda Rebecca Hughes, the couple's first child, was born in April 1960 in London. By this time, Heinemann had agreed to publish *The Colossus* and Hughes had won the prestigious Somerset Maughan Award. Plath, however, was disappointed by the lack of reaction to *The Colossus*, and while she loved her husband and new daughter, she found that the roles of mother and wife took her away from her writing.

The year 1961 was a topsy-turvy one for Sylvia Plath. It began with the sadness of a miscarriage, followed by an operation to remove an appendix. Her recovery from this she likened to a resurrection. A contract with the *New Yorker* magazine boosted her morale and she began work on her novel, *The Bell Jar*. When Plath became pregnant the couple decided to look for a house in the country, eventually moving in the autumn to Court Green in Devon. This was a rambling, crumbling old house with three acres of lawn, garden and orchard. Despite her pregnancy, the care of a young daughter and the practicalities of setting up home in an old house, Plath wrote with great energy in the first months in Devon, though the poems she completed, including 'Finisterre' and 'Mirror', are marked by a sense of threat, fear and menace.

In January 1962, Plath gave birth to her second child, Nicholas. Her experience of birth and her remembrance of her miscarriage in the previous year inform the radio play, *Three Women*, that she wrote for the BBC in the spring of 1962. The poems written later in 1962, most notably 'Elm', are dark meditations on love and self-knowledge.

By summer 1962 Plath's marriage to Hughes was beginning to unravel. Hughes became involved with Assia Wevill, the wife of a Canadian poet, and left Court Green. A holiday in Ireland in September failed to save the relationship.

Back in Court Green in October and November, Sylvia Plath, working early in the morning, wrote forty of the poems that make up the collection *Ariel*, including 'Poppies in July' and 'The Arrival of the Bee Box', published after her death. By any standards, these are remarkable poems. Writing to a friend, she said, 'I am living like a Spartan, writing through huge fevers and producing free stuff I had locked in me for years'. The strain of writing these intense, personal poems began to affect her health. Her letters to her mother from this period are touched with desperation. In November Plath decided to move back to London and found a flat in the house where W. B. Yeats had once lived. By December she had closed up Court Green and moved into her new home with her two young children. In the New Year, some of the worst weather seen in London for decades, allied to the delay in obtaining a phone and the colds and flu she and the children suffered, cast her down and left her feeling isolated. She was further disheartened by the fact that her new work was, on the whole, rejected by the editors to whom she sent it. The publication of her novel, *The Bell Jar*, under a pseudonym, did little to lift the gloom. Her final poems (including 'Child'), written in late January and early February, reveal that her will to live was almost spent. At this point Sylvia Plath sought medical help and was put on a course of anti-depressants and arrangements were made for her to see a psychiatrist. However, in the early hours of Monday morning, February 11, 1963, overcome by a despairing depression, Sylvia Plath took her own life.

Ariel, a collection of her final poems was published in 1965. Since that time, it has sold over half a million copies. Sylvia Plath's life, death and poetry have been the subject of much controversy. Understandably, given the tragic circumstances of her death, much of the response to her poetry has sought to relate her work to her life – to find clues in her poetry to explain her suicide or to attribute blame. The difference between the personality that Sylvia Plath reveals in her letters home to her mother and the darker personality of her journals has also attracted the attention of critics. Rarely has a poet left such a disputed body of work.

SOCIAL AND CULTURAL CONTEXT

The world into which Sylvia Plath was born in Boston, in 1932, was a male-dominated one. Her father ruled the family. Her mother was the wife and homemaker. Plath attended a college for girls. Here she wanted to achieve and be a perfect American girl. Magazines like *The Ladies Home Journal* defined this ideal. A woman should be a wife, a homemaker and a mother, but she was not expected to be a professional or to have her own career. She was to be respectable, that is, she was not expected to have sexual relations before marriage. There was, in this middle-class culture, a tolerance of male promiscuity but girls were expected to be modest and virginal. Not to marry was to risk being labelled 'unfeminine'. Throughout her life, Plath struggled to escape this ideal of perfection. Her letters to her mother are full of references to her attempts to make a home for herself and Ted Hughes and to win her mother's approval. She was conscious of this tendency in herself, noting in her journal: 'Old need of giving mother accomplishments, getting reward of love'.

Her biographer, Anne Stevenson, says of the letters Plath wrote to her mother:

> Letters Home *can be seen as one long projection of the 'desired image' (the required image) of herself as Eve – wife, mother, home-maker, protector of the wholesome, the good and the holy, an identity that both her upbringing and her own instinctive physical being had fiercely aspired to.*

Linda Wagner's analysis of the advertisements and contents of *The Ladies' Home Journal*, a publication to which Plath submitted her stories, makes fascinating reading:

> *Judging from illustrations throughout the magazine (1949–54), women wear either formal gowns or bathing suits; and are interested only in romance or recipes. Or, perhaps, in mother-daughter fashions. Patterns for mother-daughter 'look alike' dresses, robes and sportswear abound in many of these issues, and one must conjecture that the message is not only the natural sexual affinity but the similarity in role: whether adult or child, the female is a doll-like object, needing protection, capable of only limited activities.*

Much of Plath's poetry can be seen as a struggle to create a new identity for herself that transcended the cultural limitations imposed upon women. Given society's view of women, Plath found it difficult to find acceptance as a writer outside women's books and magazines. In her lifetime, her work won serious admiration from only a small number of people. She was more famous for being the wife of the poet Ted Hughes than for being a poet, novelist and short-story writer in her own right. Yet her ambition, dedication and determination to succeed as a writer, not to mention her talent, were as least as great, if not greater, than his.

Plath's desire to fit in at school and be an all-American girl was deepened by her consciousness of her German ancestry. Plath's use of Holocaust imagery and her reference to her father as a Nazi in her poem 'Daddy' indicate a feeling of displacement, a fear that she might, somehow, be tainted by her origins. And she employed Holocaust imagery to speak of the suffering of women. More than is sometimes acknowledged by critics, Plath was attuned, in a personal way, to the major historical issues of her time. Plath lived during the period of the Cold War and the threat of nuclear warfare between America and Russia. She was conscious of the dangers of a nuclear conflict and concerned for the future safety of her children. In a letter to her mother in December 1961, Plath wrote of these fears:

> *The reason I haven't written for so long is probably quite silly, but I got so awfully depressed two weeks ago by reading two issues of* The Nation *all about the terrifying marriage of big business and the military in America … and the repulsive shelter craze for fallout, all very factual, documented and true, that I simply couldn't sleep for nights with all the warlike talk in the papers, such as Kennedy saying Khrushchev would 'have no place to hide,' and the armed forces manuals indoctrinating soldiers about the 'inevitable' war with our 'implacable foe'…. I began to wonder if there was any point in trying to bring up children in such a mad, self-destructive world. The sad thing is that the power for destruction is real and universal.*

The fears expressed here find their way in her poetry in the terrifying imagery of her last poems.

For Sylvia Plath, the opportunity to live and study in England was a partly liberating experience. From England she could view with clarity the consumerism and militarism of American culture. However, she did not always feel at home in England and disliked the shabby inefficiency which she saw in English life. By the end of her life, Plath was caught between the two cultures, feeling ambivalent towards both. And her feelings of displacement are important in shaping the poetry she wrote.

THE ARRIVAL OF THE BEE BOX

I ordered this, this clean wood box
Square as a chair and almost too heavy to lift.
I would say it was the coffin of a midget
Or a square baby
Were there not such a din in it.   5

The box is locked, it is dangerous.
I have to live with it overnight
And I can't keep away from it.
There are no windows, so I can't see what is in there.
There is only a little grid, no exit.   10

I put my eye to the grid.
It is dark, dark,
With the swarmy feeling of African hands
Minute and shrunk for export,
Black on black, angrily clambering.   15

How can I let them out?
It is the noise that appals me most of all,
The unintelligible syllables.
It is like a Roman mob,
Small, taken one by one, but my god, together!   20

I lay my ear to furious Latin.
I am not a Caesar.
I have simply ordered a box of maniacs.
They can be sent back.
They can die, I need feed them nothing, I am the owner.   25

I wonder how hungry they are.
I wonder if they would forget me
If I just undid the locks and stood back and turned into a tree.
There is the laburnum, its blond colonnades,
And the petticoats of the cherry.   30

They might ignore me immediately
In my moon suit and funeral veil.
I am no source of honey
So why should they turn on me?
Tomorrow I will be sweet God, I will set them free.   35

The box is only temporary.

GLOSSARY

13–14 *the swarmy feeling …export*: Plath was influenced by the surrealist painter
    Giorgio de Chirico, and his use of symbols taken from the subconscious to
    create ominous, disturbing images. She was also interested in African sculpture
    and folktales. Both interests, surrealism and Africa, come together in the
    imagery of the stanza

19 *a Roman mob*: the Roman mob demanded public killings for their amusement.
    The comparison suggests the potential for destruction that the speaker senses
    in the bee box

29 *blond colonnades*: the flower-covered branches of the laburnum are compared to
    blond ringlets

30 *my moon suit and funeral veil*: Plath compares the protective suit worn by
    bee-keepers to the suit of an astronaut, while she associates the veil with
    the traditional veil worn by women mourners at a funeral

GUIDELINES

In summer 1962, Sylvia Plath and Ted Hughes decided to take up bee-keeping.
(Plath's father had been an expert on bees.) In October, following her separation
from Ted Hughes, Plath wrote a sequence of bee poems which explore the nature
of the self and self-identity, personal fears, complex relations and attitudes
towards freedom and control. Of the five poems in the sequence, 'The Arrival of
the Bee Box' is the most self-contained and narrative. The poem may be taken at
face value – it describes the arrival of the bee box and the poet's response to it.

However, the bee box is sometimes interpreted as a metaphor for the inner life of the poet.

The bee box, and all it represents, both frightens and attracts the speaker of the poem, who is fascinated with its unknown and dangerous content. As the poem progresses, the persona grows confident and determines to set the bees free. She is still fearful of what they might do and fearful, perhaps, that in freeing the bees she may lose something vital. However, if the persona risks losing something, she also has something to gain – the feeling of exercising her power in a generous way. There is a note of optimistic triumph in the final line of the poem.

If the bee box is a metaphor for what Carol Ferrier describes as 'the fertile, swarming and potentially destructive chaos that the poet sense within herself', how do we interpret the ending of the poem? Is the persona facing up to her own fears and finding a strength of purpose and resolve? Does the ending of the poem suggest that she will control her fears rather than allow her fears to control her? However, if the bees represent the inner life of the poetic persona, then the box may represent the body which contains it. 'The box is only temporary' may suggest that the inner life will be freed when it is released from the containing body – when the body dies. If the end of the poem suggests liberation, the precise nature of the liberation is unclear.

David Holbrook gives this interesting reading of the poem:

In 'The Arrival of the Bee Box' Sylvia Plath achieves a significantly developed sense of distinction between herself and the bees – she discovers resources in herself by which to deal with reality, to care for the bees, as for children. The poem's images are of a rebirth, beginning with a dead baby, ending with free bees, and the escape from death. By her recognition of the bees not merely as aspects of her identity, but as creatures in themselves, she, as 'sweet God', can release them to be themselves (as in the end she released her children).

QUESTIONS

1 Do you find the imagery of the first stanza strange, disturbing, amusing? Explain your answer.

2 'In line 7, "I have to live with it overnight", we see that the bee box represents the speaker's unconscious and is linked to the imagery of 'the dark thing that sleeps in me', referred to by the speaker in "Elm".' Do you agree with this reading of the line? Support the points you make by reference to the poem.

3 What impression is created of the box and its contents in Stanzas 3–4? What phrase or image strikes you as particularly effective?

4 In Stanza 5, the speaker seems to gain a sense of control over the box. What brings this about? What change of heart is apparent in Stanza 6?

5 In Stanzas 6–7, the speaker contemplates her own self-effacement as a way of avoiding the threat of the bees. What does this suggest about the speaker?

6 'Tomorrow I will be sweet God, I will set them free' (line 35). What is the importance of this line in the poem, and what impact does it have on you?

7 'In the poem, there is both a desire to trust the bees and a fear of trusting them, but in the end, the fear is overcome.' Do you agree with this reading of the poem? Explain your answer.

8 'The poem is remarkable for its humour; the confident handling of language; and its stanza form and organisation.' In light of this statement, comment on the form and language of the poem.

9 The critic Carole Ferrier says that: 'In this poem the box of bees becomes a metaphor for the fertile, swarming, and potentially destructive chaos that the poet senses within herself'. Comment on this assessment of the poem and the assumption that the persona of the poem is the poet.

10 In your view does the poem end on a note of optimism? Explain your answer.

CHILD

Your clear eye is the one absolutely beautiful thing.
I want to fill it with colour and ducks.
The zoo of the new

Whose names you meditate—
April snowdrop, Indian pipe,   5
Little

Stalk without wrinkle,
Pool in which images
Should be grand and classical

Not this troublous   10
Wringing of hands, this dark
Ceiling without a star.

GLOSSARY

title *Child*: Sylvia Plath's second child, Nicholas, was born in January 1962. 'Child' was
written shortly after his first birthday and less than two weeks before her death

4 *meditate*: the word means 'to reflect upon' and is used to pick up the imagery of
reflection begun in line 1, 'clear eye' and continued in line 8 with 'Pool'

5 *snowdrop*: small, white-flowering plant that blooms in spring

5 *Indian pipe*: small woodland flower

10 *troublous*: taking up the idea of classical and grand in the preceding line, Plath
uses an old-fashioned, literary word, which means agitated or unsettled

GUIDELINES

'Child' appeared in Plath's posthumous collection 'Winter Trees', published in
1971, although it was written at the end of January 1963, less than two weeks
before she took her own life at the age of thirty. The poetic persona expresses her
frustrated wishes for her child. The poem is beautifully phrased and composed.

The mother wants her child's eye to be filled with delightful things. She would like his eye to be filled with images that are 'grand and classical'. However, what he witnesses is the classical gesture of despair – the wringing of hands by his mother. This gesture is both troubled and troubling. In the poem, the power of the self is reduced to expressing its own anguish. The mother inhabits a world without hope. Her failure to fill the child's world with joy adds to her darkness and distress.

It is difficult not to read this poem in the biographical context in which it was written – two weeks before Sylvia Plath took her own life. The self that the poem presents is a self that has lost confidence in its own ability to create joy. It is a self that is shadowed by its own anguish. The mother is aware of her despair and anxious to spare her child the sight of it. The mother does not want the child's clear eye to witness the pain she endures, yet lacks the strength and self-belief – not the humour, imagination or inventiveness – to make things otherwise.

'Child' is a testimony to Sylvia Plath's skill as a poet. Every word is carefully chosen. The placing of 'Little' (line 6) and 'dark' (line 11) is perfectly judged. The despair that underlies it is managed and controlled. 'Poppies in July' and 'Mirror' also present a persona who is tormented and anguished.

QUESTIONS

1 How does the mother regard her child in line 1? What is the significance of describing the child's eye as 'clear'?

2 What does line 1 tell us about the world that the poetic persona inhabits?

3 What wish does the mother express in lines 2–3? What ideas and mood are generated by the use of the word 'zoo'?

4 What is the effect of the names recited by the mother? In what sense might the child 'meditate' the names? What is the relationship between the names and the child, in the mother's world?

5 What are the conditions in which the images in a pool might appear 'grand and classical'? Do these conditions exist in the child's life?

6 What does Stanza 4 tell us about the mother? What feeling does the mother have in relation to her child? What feeling do you have for the mother?

7 'As with all Plath's poetry, "Child" reveals her mastery of movement and phrasing.' Give your view of this assessment of the poem.

8 '"Child" can be placed with "Mirror" and "Poppies in July" in presenting an individual in tormented anguish.' Give your view of this interpretation of the poem, supporting the points you make by quotation from the poem.

ADRIENNE RICH

B. 1929

BIOGRAPHY

Adrienne Rich's most recent books of poetry are *The School Among The Ruins*: *Poems 2000–2004*, and *Fox: Poems 1998–2000* (Norton). A selection of her essays, *Arts of the Possible: Essays and Conversations*, was published in 2001. A new edition of *What is Found There: Notebooks on Poetry and Politics*, appeared in 2003. She is a recipient of the Lannan Foundation Lifetime Achievement Award, the Lambda Book Award, the Lenore Marshall/Nation Prize, the Wallace Stevens Award and the Bollingen Prize in Poetry, among other honours. She lives in California.

SOCIAL AND CULTURAL CONTEXT

As one of the leading American poets of the twentieth century, Adrienne Rich has engaged with many of the controversial ideas of her time. Almost from the beginning she saw poetry not as a means of expression for its own sake solely, but also a way in which to bring about change. She has blended poetry with politics throughout her career.

As a young woman she struggled with the conflict between the traditional roles of marriage and bringing up children, and artistic ambition. The poems in her first collection were famously praised by W. H. Auden as being 'neatly and modestly dressed; speak quietly but do not mumble; respect their elders but are not cowed by them'. This is an ironic comment in the light of her subsequent career when she became committed to what the critic Albert Gelpi calls 'the poetics of change'.

In 1950s America, as elsewhere in the western world, women poets were not encouraged to share in the same aspirations as their male counterparts. When poets such as Sylvia Plath and Adrienne Rich began to describe their experiences as women and mothers, there was as yet no wider cultural recognition that these experiences could be legitimate themes for poetry. Rich later recognised that her own work had been influenced primarily by male writers. Attitudes began to change when the women's liberation movement gathered force in the 1960s. Feminists began to enquire into the rights of women and their position in society. They analysed what they called 'the patriarchal society' in which males are the dominant power and found it wanting. Adrienne Rich was in the forefront of the movement, as her poems testify. In exploring sexual politics, Rich developed influential theories of the relationship between language, power and sexuality. These issues continue to be explored to this day.

Although it was to the women's movement that Rich gave her greatest attention, she and her husband Alfred Conrad were politically involved in the Civil Rights movement also sweeping the USA in the 1960s. Issues concerning education, especially that of Black Americans and other ethnic minorities, were highly controversial. Rich's involvement with disadvantaged students led her to further examination of the relation of language to power and the class struggle.

Throughout the 1960s, too, an anti-war movement constantly protested against American involvement in Vietnam. Rich, by this time a radical feminist fully committed to social justice, was immersed in this.

In her poems Rich records her journey with searing honesty from compliant daughter, to wife and mother, to feminist and political activist. She has not tried to diminish the emotional upheavals that accompanied her disintegrating marriage, her ex-husband's suicide, or her realisation of her lesbian sexuality. Stylistically, her poems seem to echo the tumultuous times in which she reached the peak of her career, from the formalism and control of her earlier work to the looser, more experimental style of her later poems.

Now in her seventies, Adrienne Rich continues to write, give lectures and interviews, and play an active role in political debates. Asked in 1994 if she thought writing political poetry (what the interviewer referred to as 'poetry of witness') was a good use of her time, she answered:

> I wouldn't say it isn't a good use of my time because it's really at the very core of who I am. I have to do this. This is really how I know and how I probe the world … I happen to think [poetry] makes a huge difference.

AUNT JENNIFER'S TIGERS

Aunt Jennifer's tigers prance across a screen,
Bright topaz denizens of a world of green.
They do not fear the men beneath the tree;
They pace in sleek chivalric certainty.

Aunt Jennifer's fingers fluttering through her wool   5
Find even the ivory needle hard to pull.
The massive weight of Uncle's wedding band
Sits heavily upon Aunt Jennifer's hand.

When Aunt is dead, her terrified hands will lie
Still ringed with ordeals she was mastered by.   10
The tigers in the panel that she made
Will go on prancing, proud and unafraid.

GLOSSARY

1 *prance*: to bound from the hind legs, to move proudly

2 *topaz*: a precious stone of yellow/tangerine colour

2 *denizens*: inhabitants

4 *chivalric*: knightly, courtly

10 *ordeals*: severe trials

STORM WARNINGS

The glass has been falling all the afternoon,
And knowing better than the instrument
What winds are walking overhead, what zone
Of gray unrest is moving across the land,
I leave the book upon a pillowed chair   5
And walk from window to closed window, watching
Boughs strain against the sky

And think again, as often when the air
Moves inward toward a silent core of waiting,
How with a single purpose time has traveled   10
By secret currents of the undiscerned
Into this polar realm. Weather abroad
And weather in the heart alike come on
Regardless of prediction.

Between foreseeing and averting change   15
Lies all the mastery of elements
Which clocks and weatherglasses cannot alter.
Time in the hand is not control of time,
Nor shattered fragments of an instrument
A proof against the wind; the wind will rise,   20
We can only close the shutters.

I draw the curtains as the sky goes black
And set a match to candles sheathed in glass
Against the keyhole draught, the insistent whine
Of weather through the unsealed aperture.   25
This is our sole defense against the season;
These are the things that we have learned to do
Who live in troubled regions.

GLOSSARY

1 *the glass*: the barometer

11 *undiscerned*: not seen or noticed

23 *sheathed*: enclosed in

25 *aperture*: opening

POWER

Living in the earth-deposits   of our history

Today a backhoe divulged   out of a crumbling flank of earth
one bottle   amber   perfect   a hundred-year-old
cure for fever   or melancholy   a tonic
for living on this earth   in the winters of this climate   5

Today I was reading about Marie Curie:
she must have known she suffered   from radiation sickness
her body bombarded for years   by the element
she had purified
It seems she denied to the end   10
the source of the cataracts on her eyes
the cracked and suppurating skin   of her finger-ends
till she could she no longer hold   a test-tube or a pencil

She died   a famous woman   denying
her wounds   15
denying
her wounds   came   from the same source as her power

GLOSSARY

2 *backhoe*: mechanical digger

3 *flank*: side

4 *Melancholy*: sadness, depression

6 *Marie Curie*: Polish-born chemist and physicist (1864–1934). Having come to
France and married Pierre Curie, she did pioneering research on radioactivity.
The Curies discovered radium. Marie Curie was the first person to be awarded
the Nobel Prize twice. She died of leukaemia caused by exposure to high
levels of radiation

8 *bombarded*: attacked

11 *cataracts*: a condition in which the lens of the eye becomes opaque, causing
partial blindness

12 *suppurating*: oozing pus

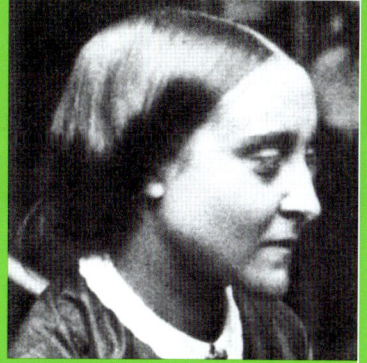

CHRISTINA ROSSETTI

1830–1894

BIOGRAPHY

Christina Rossetti was a member of one of the most famous families in Victorian England. Her father was the poet Gabriele Rossetti (1783–1854), professor of Italian at King's College from 1831. All the four children in the family became writers. Her brother, Dante Gabriel, also gained fame as a painter. Christina was educated at home by her mother, Frances Polidori, an intelligent woman, who was a devout Anglican. Christina shared her parents' interest in literature and was portrayed in the paintings and drawings of her brother and his friends. Based on the sketches made by her brother the young Christina was an attractive, even beautiful, woman.

When Gabriele Rossetti's failing health and eyesight forced him into retirement in 1853, Christina and her mother attempted to support the family by starting a day school, but had to give it up after a year or so. Like her mother, Christina was a devout Anglican and rejected two offers of marriage because of religious differences. Except for two brief visits abroad, she lived with her mother all her life.

After a serious illness in 1874, and recurrent bouts of Graves' disease, a disorder of the thyroid which altered her appearance, she rarely went outside her home. However, her circle of friends included some of the most important writers and artists of the day, including Whistler, Swinburne and Charles Dodgson (Lewis Carroll). Christina's religious feelings influenced how she led her life. For example, she gave up playing chess because she found she enjoyed winning too much!

She felt keenly the death of her beloved brother, Dante, in 1882 and, although she survived him by twelve years, she lived quietly, beset by bouts of ill health. In the weeks preceding her death, she disturbed her neighbours each night with her terrible screams of agony. Christina Rossetti died on December 29, 1894.

Christina Rossetti was composing stories and poems from before she could write, dictating her compositions to her mother. Her first collection of poetry was published in 1862, and was widely praised. It established her as a significant and distinctive voice in Victorian poetry. Several books followed: love poems and religious verse for adults, poetry and short stories for children. She wrote the words for the Christmas carol 'In the bleak midwinter' and she wrote pamphlets for the Society for Promoting Christian Knowledge. At its best, Christina Rossetti's poetry is remarkably clear and direct and her handling of form is masterful. Her recurrent themes are unhappy love, death and renunciation.

'REMEMBER ME WHEN I AM GONE AWAY'

Remember me when I am gone away,
Gone far away into the silent land;
When you can no more hold me by the hand,
Nor I half turn to go yet turning stay.
Remember me when no more day by day   5
You tell me of our future that you planned:
Only remember me; you understand
It will be late to counsel then or pray.
Yet if you should forget me for a while
And afterwards remember, do not grieve: 10
For if the darkness and corruption leave
A vestige of the thoughts that once I had,
Better by far you should forget and smile
Than that you should remember and be sad.

GLOSSARY

2 *the silent land*: usually taken as a metaphor for death. In the context of the poem as a whole, you might consider other possible meanings of the phrase

8 *counsel*: to give advice; to advise on matters of morality especially in relation to poverty, chastity and obedience

11 *the darkness and corruption*: usually interpreted as death. The speaker is referring to the darkness of her own death and the corruption of her body. However, if the terms 'darkness' and 'corruption' refer to the person she is addressing, then an entirely different reading emerges

12 *A vestige*: a trace; a hint; a slight amount of something that was once plentiful

GUIDELINES

'Remember me' was written in 1849 when Rossetti was just 19 years old. In the poem, a woman addresses her beloved before her death and urges him to remember her, or to forget her, if remembering makes him sad.

It is unwise to identify the speaker in the poem with the poet. This, in common with other poems that Rossetti wrote at this time, is a dramatic monologue. The most notable feature of the poem is the ambivalence which the speaker reveals towards the person she addresses. For some readers, the poem is marked by an unexpected irony and a note of anger. The speaker may well welcome death as a release from the lover's grasp and insensitivity, from the future that *he* planned for them both. This reading is dependent upon the tone in which certain key lines and phrases are read. Lines 3–4, 6, 8 and 11 are all open to different interpretations.

The dramatic situation (the speaker addressing her beloved before her death) is reminiscent of the poetry of Emily Dickinson. In 'After Death', another poem which Rossetti wrote in 1849, the speaker lies on a bed with a shroud on her face, observing the surroundings before her burial. It has a similar ambivalent quality to 'Remember me': 'He did not love me living; but once dead / He pitied me; and very sweet it is / To know he still is warm tho' I am cold.'

'Remember me' has little of the passionate declarations of love associated with Victorian love poetry. Instead it has a clarity and directness, an unsentimental, clear-eyed detachment that suggests that, for the speaker, her feelings of love have cooled, if not disappeared. Some traditional views of Rossetti have described her poetry as sincere and superficial. Recent criticism by feminist scholars suggest that Rossetti's poetry is far more subtle in its effects and intentions than has been understood or appreciated. 'Remember me', for example, is based on a paradox. The poem begins with an invitation to remember and concludes with an exhortation to forget!

'Remember me' is remarkable for the ease with which Rossetti rhymes and makes the thought fit the sonnet shape, while maintaining a dramatic voice, which gives the poem a contemporary feel.

Virigina Woolf's estimation of Christina Rossetti as a poet may help in reading 'Remember me':

You were not a pure saint by any means. You pulled legs; you tweaked noses. You were at war with all humbug and pretense. Modest as you were, still you were drastic, sure of your gift, convinced of your vision … in a word, you were an artist.

The speaker of the poem may well share Rossetti's impatience with pretence and though she speaks simply and directly, there is a strength and confidence in her voice.

QUESTIONS

1 What is the speaker of the poem asking the 'you' to do after her death?
2 How does the speaker feel about the 'you' of the poem? What lines best reveal her feelings?
3 'It will be late to counsel then or pray.' What impression of the 'you' do you form from this line? Explain your answer. Where else do you think the character of the 'you' is suggested?
4 Describe a dramatic situation which you think fits the poem. Give a description of the speaker and the 'you' to whom she addresses her words.
5 Prepare two readings of the poem which offer contrasting views of the relationship between the speaker of the poem and the 'you'.
6 The poem has a number of opposites or contrasts. Identify these and comment on them.
7 What is your impression of the speaker of the poem? Support the points you make by quotation form the poem.
8 Is 'Remember me' a well-made poem? Support the points you make by quotation from the poem.
9 Do you like the poem? Explain your answer.

SIEGFRIED SASSOON

1886–1967

BIOGRAPHY

Sassoon was a member of a distinguished Jewish family which made its mark in English politics and finance. He was brought up as an English country gentleman, educated at a leading English grammar school and at Cambridge, from where he was sent down without taking a degree. Before the First World War he enjoyed tennis, foxhunting and writing poetry. When war broke out he enlisted and was posted to France as a junior officer. He displayed uncommon gallantry, was twice wounded and won the Military Cross. He was invalided home in 1917, and in protest against the inhumanity of war, announced publicly that he would not serve again. For this courageous stand he expected to be court-martialled, but was sent to a sanatorium instead. He went back to France, was again wounded, and ended the war as a Captain. In 1928, he published anonymously his prose classic, *Memoirs of a Fox-Hunting Man*, which provides a stimulating account of his war experiences. His war poems are often savagely satirical, exposing the sickening reality of war in the trenches. His main targets are complacent politicians and senior officers, whose incompetence and cynicism consigned millions of common soldiers to a living death. Although Sassoon wrote poetry after the war, his characteristic achievement belongs to the wartime period.

ON PASSING THE NEW MENIN GATE

Who will remember, passing through this Gate,
The unheroic Dead who fed the guns?
Who shall absolve the foulness of their fate—
Those doomed, conscripted, unvictorious ones?
Crudely renewed, the Salient holds its own.   5
Paid are its dim defenders by this pomp;
Paid, with a pile of peace-complacent stone,
The armies that endured that sullen swamp.

Here was the world's worst wound. And here with pride
"Their name liveth forever," the Gateway claims.   10
Was ever an immolation so belied
As these intolerably nameless names?
Well might the Dead that struggled in the slime
Rise and deride this sepulchre of crime.

GLOSSARY

title and line 1 *Gate*: the Menin Gate, in Flanders, Belgium, is an impressive memorial to massive numbers of British soldiers killed during the third battle of Ypres. This battle began on 31 July 1917, and lasted three months. The new Menin Gate was unveiled in 1927

2 *unheroic Dead*: British political and military leaders hailed the soldiers who died in battle as heroes. Sassoon's point is that war is far from being heroic. The battles in which the soldiers perished were sordid, bloody affairs, fought in muddy fields and filthy trenches

3 *absolve*: grant forgiveness for

5 *crudely renewed*: part of the memorial consisted of a crude reconstruction of part of the battlefield

5 *the Salient holds its own*: a Salient is a piece of land that juts out to form an angle. Here it is an outward bulge in a military line, which British troops had to defend with their lives. After death they are buried within the Salient, and so it can be said to hold its own

6 *dim defenders*: the defenders are 'dim' because they are obscure, because they are covered by the earth, and perhaps because they were stupid enough to fight for ruthless leaders

7 *peace-complacent stone*: the only reward the soldiers get is a stone-built monument erected by complacent (self-satisfied) survivors

8 *swamp*: the soldiers fought in mud and slime

9 *the world's worst wound*: the most violent assault on civilisation

11 *was ever an immolation so belied*: the poet wonders whether such human sacrifice was ever so casually treated

11 *immolation*: sacrificial slaughter

12 *intolerably nameless names*: the monument does not name any of the individuals who were sacrificed in the battle. The poet finds it intolerable that so many who died needlessly are now forgotten

13-14 *Well might … crime*: no one could blame the dead soldiers if they rose from their graves to condemn this monument to their slaughter, which was a crime committed against them by those who led them into battle. Sassoon may have in mind Christ's reference to hypocrites as 'whited sepulchres'

GUIDELINES

The poem deals with what Sassoon thinks of as a futile, hypocritical attempt to commemorate the sacrifice of hundreds of thousands of British and Irish soldiers in and around Ypres in 1917. The three battles of Ypres, which formed part of the British offensive in Flanders, resulted in 324,000 British casualties. German casualties amounted to 202,000. Sassoon's poem focuses particularly on the third of these battles, popularly known as the Battle of Passchendaele, and described at the time by the British Prime Minister, Lloyd George, as the battle of the mud. The torrential rains of August 1917 turned the battlefield into a sea of mud. Soldiers struggled to advance up to their waists in slime. The British advanced four miles, and they evacuated the Salient when the Germans took the offensive in March 1918. The British tanks and artillery were useless in the mud of Flanders.

To understand this poem, one must take account of Sassoon's background and his experience of war. He served as an infantry officer in the First World War. Like many young fighting men of his generation, he had been taught by those who organised and backed the war to regard it as noble and heroic enterprise waged for a good cause. The horrible reality of war for those who fought shocked and repelled him, and inspired a series of bitter, often savage, anti-war poems. He was twice wounded seriously while serving in France. While still in the army, he published two collections of anti-war poetry, *The Old Huntsman* (1917) and *Counterattack* (1918). At the same time, he publicly asserted his pacifism. The authorities were fearful that the anti-war publicity generated by Sassoon, a war-hero who had been awarded the Military Cross for gallantry, might undermine the war-effort. His reluctance to fight was attributed to shell-shock, and he was confined to a sanitorium.

On Passing the New Menin Gate is an effective poem of protest. It is based on an ironic contrast between the glorification of war by those who do not have to take part in it, and the reality of war as this is experienced by the unfortunate volunteers and conscripts, many of whom are doomed to die anonymously. The main emphasis of the poem is on the real meaning of war for those who are forced to take part in it. The fate of hundreds of young conscripts is to be slaughtered in the mud. Their reward is a stone monument dominating a landscape of mass graves ('these intolerably nameless names').

Those responsible for erecting the monument want to suggest that the dead soldiers it honours (or dishonours as Sassoon believes) sacrificed their lives for a great ideal. Hence the inscription on the gateway, 'their name liveth forever'. But, as Sassoon argues in the poem, this inscription tells a lie. Their names do not live forever, because they are a massive dead collection of 'nameless names'. In its most fundamental aspect, war is a matter of leaders, many of them incompetent, converting young men into cannon-fodder, into 'the unheroic Dead who fed the guns'. The New Menin Gate is a monument not to the memory of heroes, but to the criminal folly of political and military leaders who sent young men to their deaths. This is why Sassoon refers to the memorial as 'this sepulchre of crime', and why he is able to suggest that if the soldiers could rise from the dead and speak, they would express their contempt for the 'pile of peace-complacent stone' erected in their memory.

QUESTIONS

1 Irony involves a contrast between what is said and what is meant, between the gesture and the reality. Examine some instances of irony in the poem.

2 Discuss the tone of the poem.

3 How does Sassoon compare the reward given to the soldiers with what they earned through their suffering?

4 The poem has three major questions. What answers does the poet expect us to give to these questions?

5 Is this poem an absolute condemnation of war?

6 Write your own response to the poem. Has it a meaning for our time?

WILLIAM SHAKESPEARE

1564–1616

BIOGRAPHY

One of Shakespeare's eighteenth-century editors, George Steevens, claimed that:

> all that we know of Shakespeare is that he was born at Stratford-on-Avon;
> married and had children there; went to London, where he commenced [as an]
> actor, and wrote plays and poems; returned to Stratford, made his will, and died.

Even in the eighteenth century, more of Shakespeare's life story was known than Steevens acknowledged, but there are still very large gaps indeed in his biography, in spite of centuries of patient and diligent scholarly effort.

Much of what passes for Shakespeare's biography is, in fact, largely a tissue of documentary records, mainly of trivial facts; traditions, legends and anecdotes, often of doubtful value; references to Shakespeare in the works of his contemporaries and, most unsatisfactory of all, assumptions based on passages in the plays and sonnets. In the absence of a substantial volume of undisputed facts, biographers are often forced to fall back on 'perhaps', 'it is probable', 'it is likely', 'it is almost certain', and so on.

There are, however, lives of Shakespeare that run to several hundred pages. It is known that Shakespeare's father, John, came into Stratford from a neighbouring farm in the 1550s, practised a variety of trades, achieved prosperity, owned property and became a leading citizen of the town, which at that time had a population of about one thousand. Shakespeare was christened at the parish church at Stratford on 26 April, 1564. It can be taken for granted that he attended the local grammar school, only half a mile from his home, until he was sixteen. In Shakespeare's day, grammar school education was focused almost exclusively on the study of the Latin language and its literature; students also learned rhetoric, which is the art of public speaking. In 1582, Shakespeare married Anne Hathaway. She was twenty-six; he was eighteen. They had three children. Their only son, Hamnet, died in 1596, aged eleven. No record of Anne Hathaway exists between the baptism of her children and the drafting of her husband's will in 1616, the year of his death, when he left her his second-best bed.

By the 1590s, Shakespeare had become a rising dramatist. By 1595, he was a sharer in an acting company. Two years later, he was able to buy New Place, the second largest property in Stratford. Between 1590 and 1603 he spent most of his time in London, writing plays, arranging for their performance and occasionally acting in them. Of the twenty-six plays he wrote during this period, *Hamlet* (1601) is the most celebrated. Between 1603 and his death thirteen years later in 1616, Shakespeare wrote his four other tragic masterpieces: *Othello* (1604), *King Lear* (1606), *Macbeth* (1606) and *Anthony and Cleopatra* (1607). The sonnets were published in 1609, but were almost certainly written over a decade before. His great plays were all first performed at the Globe theatre in London, in which he was a shareholder.

Shakespeare combined supreme creative ability with practical instincts and an impressive business sense. Records from the last decade of his life show him acquiring considerable property in and around his place of birth, and shrewdly protecting his legal interests there. In addition to houses, he purchased over one hundred acres of farmland and an interest in tithes which guaranteed a substantial income. When debts owing to him remained unpaid, he was quick to sue the defaulters, even in petty cases. Three years before he died, he bought a house in London as an investment.

Shakespeare appears to have taken far less interest in the fate of his writings than in his property and investment income. He did not oversee the publication of the editions of his plays published during his lifetime. These are carelessly printed and contain many errors. The sonnets were published without his supervision or consent. At his death, much of his most celebrated work was still in manuscript form, and remained so until his friends and colleagues John Heminges and Henry Condell published his complete plays in 1623 in an edition now known as the *First Folio*. This substantial volume contains all the plays now attributed to Shakespeare, except *Pericles*.

FEAR NO MORE THE HEAT O' TH' SUN

Guiderius	Fear no more the heat o' th' sun,
	Nor the furious winter's rages,
	Thou thy worldly task has done,
	Home art gone and ta'en thy wages.
	Golden lads and girls all must, 5
	As chimney-sweepers, come to dust.
Arviragus	Fear no more the frown o' th' great,
	Thou art past the tyrant's stroke,
	Care no more to clothe and eat,
	To thee the reed is as the oak: 10
	The sceptre, learning, physic, must
	All follow this and come to dust.
Gui.	Fear no more the lightening-flash.
Arv.	Nor th' all-dreaded thunder-stone.
Gui.	Fear not slander, censure rash. 15
Arv.	Thou hast finish'd joy and moan.
Both.	All lovers young, all lovers must
	Consign to thee and come to dust.
Gui.	No exorciser harm thee!
Arv.	Nor no witchcraft charm thee! 20
Gui.	Ghost unlaid forbear thee!
Arv.	Nothing ill come near thee!
Both.	Quiet consummation have,
	And renowned be thy grave!

2 *rages*: storms

8 *tyrant's stroke*: the power of a wicked, unjust dictatorial ruler to inflict the severest punishment, even death

11 *sceptre*: the king's staff of office, here standing for the king himself

learning: the scholar

physic: medicine, here referring to the doctor

14 *thunder-stone*: a meteorite, a mass of solid matter whose fall from the sky is accompanied by a sound like thunder

15 *slander*: a false, malicious statement intended to injure someone's reputation

censure rash: blame or condemnation without sufficient evidence

16 *moan*: complaint, lament

18 *Consign to thee*: agree to enlist or sign up in the ranks of death

19 *exorciser*: a person capable of conjuring up spirits

21 *Ghost … thee*: may you be left alone by spirits not yet banished or laid to rest

22 *ill*: evil

23 *consummation*: death

24 *renowned*: made famous, honoured

GUIDELINES

This song is taken from *Cymbeline*, a late play by Shakespeare. Cymbeline is the King of Britain. His two sons, Guiderius and Arviragus, are stolen from him and brought up in Wales by one of his nobles whom he has wronged. His daughter Imogen remains at his court, falls in love with Posthumus, the son of one of his warriors, and marries him. When Imogen's mother dies, Cymbeline marries a wicked widow with a brutal, foolish son named Cloten. The new queen decides that Cloten should marry Imogen. When it is discovered that Imogen has married Posthumus, the latter is banished. A wicked character named Iachimo convinces Posthumus that Imogen has been unfaithful to him in his absence. Mad with rage, Posthumus instructs his servant Pisanio to take Imogen to Wales and kill her. Moved by Imogen's goodness and innocence, Pisanio spares her, giving her a medicinal drug to comfort her. This drug turns out to be a powerful sleeping draught. Imogen puts on boy's clothes, and finds the cave where her unknown brothers, Guiderius and Arviragus, live. Imogen introduces herself to them as Fidele, a young man bound for Milford Haven. They show great kindness to their new acquaintance. When Imogen takes the drug given to her by Pisanio, she falls into a death-like sleep. Guiderius and Arviragus, thinking her dead, cover her with flowers and sing this lament.

The comments of Guiderius and Arviragus on the supposedly dead Fidele, whom they do not recognise as their sister, provide a moving context for the lament. Guiderius hopes that Fidele/Imogen may not, after all, be dead. He says (in Act 4, Scene 2, lines 216–19):

> *Why, he but sleeps:*
> *If he be gone he'll make his grave a bed.*
> *With female fairies will his tomb be haunted*
> *And worms will not come to thee.*

The events of the play unfold to make the beautiful lament of Imogen's brothers premature. *Cymbeline* is a romance, not a tragedy. The good characters are finally rewarded and the evil Cloten is decapitated. Imogen forgives her deceived and repentant husband, Posthumus. Cymbeline has his sons restored to him and all ends in happiness and peace.

The impulse behind this lament (or dirge) is to draw whatever consolation is possible from death, so that those who are left behind may not succumb to absolute despair. The varieties of consolation to be drawn from the event are expressed in the first four lines of each of the first three stanzas. In each of these groups of lines, the main idea is that the dead person is beyond the reach of misery, danger or misfortune, and is thus to be envied. The multiple dangers from which the dead are free include bad weather, the displeasure of great people, the danger to life posed by tyrants, the struggle to provide for bodily needs, the threat of sudden disaster, slander and criticism. This catalogue of mortal ills will no longer have meaning to the dead, thus inspiring the thought that death is to be welcomed rather than feared.

The dirge balances against this idea of welcome death another commonplace: that death is inevitable. This is expressed in the final two lines of the first three stanzas. The idea that death comes to all human beings, whatever their rank, is driven home with sad directness by the rhyming of 'dust' and 'must' at the end of each of the three stanzas. The final six lines are a series of charms and spells, invoking protection for the departed spirit from evil influences.

LANGUAGE

Much of the power and interest of the song derives from the way in which the dominant ideas are brought to life in terms of concrete illustrations. Instead of generalising about the threats posed to everyday mortals by those in power,

Shakespeare suggests their menace in 'the *frown* o' the great' and 'the tyrant's *stroke*'. People and their offices are identified by reference to significant items associated with them: kings, learned men and doctors become 'sceptre, learning, physic'. The final two lines of the first stanza are particularly impressive: 'Golden lads and girls all must / As chimney-sweepers, come to dust'. The essential contrast here is between privileged boys and girls endowed with both beauty and wealth ('golden' suggests both the glow of youth and beauty and the possession of wealth and privilege) and those who, like chimney-sweeps, are neither beautiful nor rich. There is a disturbing pun on 'dust' in line 6. By virtue of their trade, chimney-sweepers, who were boys, necessarily 'came to dust', but the real purpose of the lines is to remind us that the most beautiful and prosperous youths and maidens have no better defence against becoming dust in the grave than have the poor dusty chimney-sweeps.

QUESTIONS

1 Two ways of looking at death are considered in this song. Describe them.
2 Examine the way in which the images in this song help to convey contrasting attitudes to death.
3 Discuss the relationship between general statements and the way in which these are brought home to the imagination by Shakespeare.
4 Consider the song as an illustration of Shakespeare's fondness for wordplay.
5 Is this an entirely sad poem?

PERCY BYSSHE SHELLEY

1792–1822

BIOGRAPHY

Shelley was born in Sussex. He had a privileged childhood. From his earliest years he was rebellious, showing little respect for authority or convention. At Eton he was known as 'mad Shelley' and the 'Eton Atheist'. At Oxford he was influenced by radical authors and dedicated himself to a campaign against Christianity. He was the joint author of a pamphlet called *The Necessity of Atheism* and was expelled from Oxford for refusing to discuss its contents with the university authorities. He eloped to Scotland with the sixteen-year-old Harriet Westbrook, whose unhappiness at school drove him to rescue her. Shelley regarded schools as centres of oppression.

Shelley's lifelong vocation was to emancipate the human spirit from the bondage of all kinds of authority and convention. In Dublin in 1812, he distributed tracts calling for Catholic emancipation from the Penal Laws and for the repeal of the Act of Union. Back in England, he attacked Christianity and defended the right of free speech. In 'Queen Mab', a poem which appeared in 1813, he denounced kings and priests as agents of divine tyranny. He soon tired of his young wife and formed an attachment to Mary Wollstonecraft, the sixteen-year-old daughter of the radical author William Godwin, who disapproved of marriage as a constraint on human liberty. In 1816, when Harriet drowned herself, Shelley immediately married Mary, whose principal claim to fame was to rest on her authorship of *Frankenstein* (1818).

In 1818, Shelley left England for Italy, where he spent the rest of his life. There he composed all the poetry for which he is now remembered: 'Ode to the West Wind', 'To Liberty', 'The Masque of Anarchy' and some fine sonnets, including 'Ozymandias'.

In August 1822, Shelley was drowned at sea and his body was cremated. He never abandoned his radical impulses and remained an anarchist to the end. His political and religious views, together with his unconventional private life, have tended to obscure his achievements as a poet, which soon earned him a secure place, along with Wordsworth, Coleridge, Keats, Blake and Byron, among the great English Romantics.

OZYMANDIAS

I met a traveller form an antique land
Who said: Two vast and trunkless legs of stone
Stand in the desert … Near them, on the sand,
Half sunk, a shattered visage lies, whose frown,
And wrinkled lip, and sneer of cold command,   5
Tell that its sculptor well those passions read
Which yet survive, stamped on these lifeless things,
The hand that mocked them, and the heart that fed:
And on the pedestal these words appear:
'My name is Ozymandias, king of kings: 10
Look on my works, ye Mighty, and despair!'
Nothing beside remains. Round the decay
Of that colossal wreck, boundless and bare
The lone and level sands stretch far away.

GLOSSARY

title *Ozymandias*: The statue in the poem, which stands in the desert at Thebes in Egypt, is that of Rameses II. Rameses was given the name Ozymandias by a Greek historian

1 *antique land*: a country which boasted an ancient civilisation

4 *visage*: face

6–8 *Tell that its sculptor … fed*: the sculptor has expressed the passions of Ozymandias on the face of the statue. These passions, stamped on stone, still survive the hand of the sculptor and the king

8 *The hand that mocked them*: the hand is that of the sculptor. He has mockingly recorded the cruel passions of Ozymandias on the face of the statue

8 *the heart that fed*: the heart is that of Ozymandias. Passions, emotions and feelings were supposed to have their origin in the heart

11 *Look on my works, ye Mighty, and despair!*: when Ozymandias ordered this inscription, he must have hoped that even the mightiest kings would feel despair when they saw his achievements, since they could never hope to equal them. Now that these works have all but vanished, the inscription has a different meaning. Rulers and great men of the world looking at the pedestal now will feel despair that their best achievements will meet the same fate as those of Ozymandias

GUIDELINES

The setting of this poem is the Middle-Eastern desert. Shelley wrote it during a period when there was a growing interest throughout Europe in the antiquities of the Middle East, and particularly those of Egypt. The statue described in the poem is based on the colossal statue of the ancient Egyptian ruler Rameses II.

Many of Shelley's contemporaries were overwhelmed by the magnificence of Egyptian monuments, which were many times larger than life, and by the contemplation of the power and prestige enjoyed by kings of antiquity. Shelley, however, had a different view. He was an anarchist, opposed on principle to kingship and to all forms of tyranny, which he regarded as hostile to the welfare of the human race. This attitude helps to explain his attitude to the ruined statue described in the poem. For him, the contemplation of the wrecked statue of a once magnificent monarch is not an occasion for regret or pity. Instead, it is a source of gratification to him that even the mightiest tyrannies are doomed to decline and fall, the only memorial of their greatness being some large fragments of stone in a desert which has buried all the other evidence of the past.

SUBJECT MATTER

The speaker of the poem is recording the experience of a traveller who has been visiting a country in which the remains of an ancient civilisation are still to be found. The traveller has been particularly impressed by the sight of two enormous legs of stone, the only parts of a once great statue standing after thousands of years. The trunk of the statue is no longer to be seen. On the desert sand, half-buried, the traveller finds the enormous head of the statue. He is struck by the expression on its face. It is not a happy or a pleasant expression. The frown, the wrinkled lip and the sneer are those of a tyrant who was used to giving commands and having these commands obeyed. The face suggests a cold heart and a pitiless nature. It also suggests that the tyrant had a high sense of his own importance and that he felt contempt for those he ruled. The sculptor who made the statue was highly skilled. He could read the heart of the tyrant and understand the passions that this heart fed: the cruelty, the anger, the lust for power and authority. In showing these passions on the face of the statue, the sculptor was at the same time mocking them.

The tyrant's sense of his own importance is suggested by the inscription on the base of the statue. The tyrant boasts of being not merely a king, but 'king of kings'. The inscription invites the other great men who look at the statue, and at the other great works found throughout the tyrant's kingdom, to despair of ever achieving such magnificence. The tyrant would like everyone to see him as the envy of the world. Nothing, however, remains for anyone to envy. The once proud statue is a great ruin. The tyrant's kingdom, with all its magnificence, has vanished, buried under an endless stretch of desert. The words on the pedestal take on a new, disturbing meaning.

FORM OF THE POEM

The poem is a sonnet. Shelley makes a broad division between the first eight lines and the last six. This division is an important structural feature. In the first eight lines we are invited to imagine a desert scene at the centre of which are the remains of a great statue. The emphasis is on description. The final six lines suggest a reflection on what has gone before. Shelley uses them to draw a moral from what the traveller has seen. The emptiness of pomp and power are revealed. The boastful inscription is mocked by the passage of time as well as by the boundless desert. The moving description in the final lines encourages us to reflect that time does not distinguish between the great and the humble: the desert eventually covers all.

THEMES

Various connected themes may be traced in the sonnet. One prominent theme is the destructive power of time, also a common theme in Shakespeare's sonnets. In 'Ozymandias', time is seen to mock the greatest achievements and hopes of the world's most powerful men.

Another theme of the sonnet is the emptiness of power. The tyrant Ozymandias once lorded it over kings and made slaves of his subjects. He could boast of immense achievements. Now no trace remains of him or his achievements except a broken statue in the desert.

A third theme is a favourite one among poets – the immortality of art. Human life passes away, but civilisations are remembered mainly in their works of art. Here all that survives of an impressive ancient civilisation is a work of sculpture. Without the broken statue and its inscription, even the name of the great Ozymandias would be lost to memory. As it is, his cruel passions have been made immortal through the art of the sculptor.

IRONY

There is a fundamental irony in the poem. All irony involves some form of contrast. The great contrast of this poem is between the magnificent works which once proudly dominated the desert and the poor remains of those ruined pieces of sculpture which the traveller contemplates. A powerful kind of irony is centred on Ozymandias. One must assume that at the height of his power, thousands of years ago, he gave orders for the inscription on the pedestal: 'My name is Ozymandias, king of kings, / Look on my works, ye Mighty, and despair'. When the inscription was carved by the sculptor, it was intended to glorify Ozymandias. It was meant to convey to other rulers that they should despair of ever creating such mighty works as Ozymandias had. Now, thousands of years later, the inscription takes on a new, ironic meaning. If modern rulers read it, they will indeed despair, but their despair will not be caused by envy of Ozymandias. Instead, they will feel despair at the thought that even the works of the mightiest kings are doomed to meet the same fate as those meted out at the orders of Ozymandias.

There is irony in the notion that if Ozymandias could return to the scene of his former greatness, he would find a totally new meaning in the original inscription. He himself would be the one to feel despair rather than inspire it in others. Irony can be found in the following:

> Half sunk, a shattered visage lies, whose frown
> And wrinkled lip, and sneer of cold command,
> Tell that its sculptor well those passions read
> Which yet survive, stamped on thee lifeless things,
> The hand that mocked them, and the heart that fed.

The sculptor's hand once ironically mocked the king's passions by depicting them on the statue's face. The king's heart once fuelled the same passions. It is ironic that these passions have survived both sculptor and king.

LANGUAGE AND IMAGERY

The language of the sonnet is mainly descriptive, and impressive in the simplicity of its diction. Shelley is content to set a scene, describe the face of the statue and record the words of the inscription. He allows the imagination of the reader to do the rest. The most impressive piece of description is at the end: 'Round the decay / Of that colossal wreck, boundless and bare / The lone and level sands stretch far away'. Here the sounds of the words are a perfect echo of their meanings. The slow rhythms and broad vowels, especially in the final line, help to convey a remarkable impression of endless stretches of empty desert.

QUESTIONS

1 Discuss the use of contrast as a structural feature of 'Ozymandias'.
2 Describe the speaker's attitude to what he is recording in the poem. How is this attitude reflected in the tone of his comments?
3 Is it possible to feel pity for Ozymandias?
4 Consider the significance of the desert landscape as part of the meaning of the poem.
5 Discuss the sonnet as a meditation on the theme of time, the great enemy.

RICHARD WILBUR

B. 1921

BIOGRAPHY

Richard Wilbur was born in New York in 1921. He was educated at Amherst College and Harvard University. The son of a commercial artist, Wilbur was interested in painting in his youth, but he eventually chose to become a writer, possibly because of the strong literary influence of his maternal grandfather and great-grandfather, both of whom were editors. His writing career began after he had served in the US Army during the Second World War.

He has been a lecturer, professor of English and writer-in-residence at a number of universities in the USA, including Harvard, Wellesley College, Massachusetts and Smith College, Massachusetts. In 1961 he was the cultural exchange representative of the USA in the former Soviet Union. He has translated French classical plays, in particular those of Racine and Molière, which have been successfully produced in New York. He is also a distinguished critic. Wilbur has won many major literary awards, including the Pulitzer prize. In 1987–88 he was named as the United States' Poet Laureate. His *New and Collected Poems* was published in 1989.

THE PARDON

My dog lay dead five days without a grave
In the thick of summer, hid in a clump of pine
And a jungle of grass and honey-suckle vine.
I who had loved him while he kept alive
Went only close enough to where he was   5
To sniff the heavy honeysuckle-smell
Twined with another odor heavier still
And hear the flies' intolerable buzz.
Well, I was ten and very much afraid.
In my kind world the dead were out of range   10
And I could not forgive the sad or strange
In beast or man. My father took the spade
And buried him. Last night I saw the grass
Slowly divide (it was the same scene
But now it glowed a fierce and mortal green)   15
And saw the dog emerging. I confess
I felt afraid again, but still he came
In the carnal sun, clothed in a hymn of flies,
And death was breeding in his lively eyes.
I started in to cry and call his name,   20
Asking forgiveness of his tongueless head.
..I dreamt the past was never past redeeming:
But whether this was false or honest dreaming
I beg death's pardon now. And mourn the dead.

GLOSSARY

15 *mortal*: deathly

18 *carnal*: fleshy; here, possibly in Shakespearean sense of *murderous*.

GUIDELINES

The poet remembers a childhood experience which he found traumatic, namely the death of his pet dog. He confesses to us that he left the dog unburied for five days during a hot summer. Clearly he feels sorry and guilty for this, even after all this time. In the poem he recaptures the scene in strong sensuous images that make us see, hear and smell the situation.

In the third stanza he comments on the event. As an adult now he knows that his failure to deal with the dog's death was due to childish innocence. Death had no place in his 'kind world'. He hints too at another emotion he felt at the time: anger at the dog for having died. He found it hard to 'forgive' him.

His father's burial of the dog might appear to have brought the experience to an end. But the poet reveals that it has haunted him ever since. Now an adult, he dreams of his dog in a similar situation and yet changed, as is the way in dreams. As in dreams, too, everything – colours, the dog himself – is exaggerated. His old fear returns.

This time, however, he overcomes his fear and begs the dog's pardon.

In the last three lines he suggests a possible interpretation of the dream. Mistakes may be put right; the past may be atoned for. Although the poet does not know exactly whether this is true – is it 'false' or 'honest' dreaming? – it is an essentially optimistic and comforting moment of insight, especially if applied to human relationships. What we can certainly do, the poem suggests, is express regret for the mistakes we have made, no matter how late it is.

QUESTIONS

1 Would you agree that the child's fear of his dead dog is very well portrayed in the poem?

2 Apart from fear, what other feelings does the child experience?

3 What sort of childhood did the speaker have, in your opinion?

4 Is the dream sequence convincing, in your opinion? Support your view with reference to the poem.

5 'I dream the past was never past redeeming.' Would you agree that this is the main idea or theme of the poem?

6 How does this poem make you feel? Give a reason for your answer.

7 Why did the poet choose the title 'The Pardon' for this poem? Refer to the poem in your answer.

8 You want to make a short film of this poem. Describe the sort of atmosphere you would like to create. And say what music, sound effects and images you would use.

READING
UNSEEN POETRY

Reading a poem is an activity in which your mind, your beliefs and your feelings are called into play. As you read, you work to create the poem's meaning from the words and images offered to you by the poet. And the process takes a little time, so be patient. However, the fact that poems are generally short – much shorter than most stories, for example – allows you to read and reread a poem many times over.

Begin with the title. What expectations does it set up in you? What does it remind you of? As you read a poem, jot down your responses. These jottings may take the form of words or phrases from the poem which you feel are important, although you may not be able to say why this is so. Write questions, teasing out the literal meaning of a word or a phrase. Write notes or commentaries as you go, expressing your understanding. Record your feelings. Record your resistance to, or your approval of, any aspect of the poem – its statements, the choice of words, the imagery, the tone, the values it expresses.

Jot down any association brought to mind by any element of the poem, such as a word. Note any ideas suggested by any part of a poem – a word, a phrase, an image, the rhythm or tone, or the title. Be alert to combinations of words and patterns of repetition. Look for those words or images that carry emotional or symbolic force. Try to understand their effect. Note down other poems which the unseen poem reminds you of. In this way, you create a territory in which the poem can be read and understood.

Don't feel that you have to supply all the answers asked of you by a poem. In a class situation, confer with your fellow students. Words and images will resonate in different ways for different people. Readers bring their own style, ideas and experiences to every encounter with a poem. Sharing ideas and adopting a collaborative approach to the reading of a new poem will open out the poem's possibilities beyond what you, or any individual, will achieve alone.

Poems frequently work by way of hints, suggestions or associations. The unstated may be as important as the stated. Learn to live with ambiguity. Learn to enjoy the uncertainty of poetry. Don't be impatient if a poem doesn't 'make sense' to you. Most readers interpret and work on poems with more success than they know or admit! Learning to recognise your own competence and trusting in it is an important part of reading poems in a fruitful way. Remember that reading is an active process and that your readings are provisional and open to reconsideration.

In an examination, you will not be able to talk with your fellow students or return to the poem many times, over a couple of days. Trust yourself. In an examination the poem may be new to you, but the reading of poems is not. Draw on your experience of creating meaning. Poetry works to reveal the world in new ways. D. H. Lawrence said: 'The essential quality of poetry is that it makes a new effort of attention and "discovers" a new world within the known world'. In an examination, you are looking to show how a poem, and your reading of it, presents a new view of the world. Read the poem over, noting and jotting as you do so, and then focus on different aspects of the poem. The questions set on the poem will help direct your attention.

Here are some suggested ways into a poem. They are not exhaustive or definitive.

THE WORDS OF THE POEM

Remember that every word chosen by a poet suggests that another word was rejected.

In poetry some words are so charged with meaning that literal or everyday meaning gives way to their figurative or poetic meaning. Often there are one or two words in a poem that carry a weight of meaning: these words can be read in a variety of ways that open up the poem for you.

Here are some questions you can ask:

1 Are the words in the poem simple or complex, concrete or abstract?
2 How are they clustered into phrases?
3 Are there any obvious patterns of word usage, for example words that refer to colours, or verbs that suggest energy and force?
4 Is there a pattern in the descriptive words used by the poet?
5 Are there key words – words that carry a symbolic or emotional force – or a clear set of associations? (Does the poet play with these associations by calling them into question or subverting them?)
6 Do patterns of words establish any contrasts or oppositions, for example night and day, winter and summer, joy and sorrow, love and death?

THE MUSIC AND MOVEMENT OF THE POEM

In relation to the sounds and rhythms of the poem, note such characteristics as the length of the lines or the presence or absence of rhyme. Consider how sound patterns add to the poem's texture and meaning. For example, do the sound patterns create a sense of hushed stillness or an effect of forceful energy?

Ask yourself some or all of the following questions:

1 What is the pattern of line length in the poem?
2 What is the pattern of rhyme?
3 Is there a pattern to vowel sounds and length? What influence might this have on the rhythm of the poem or the feelings conveyed by it?
4 Are there patterns of consonant sounds, including alliteration? What is their effect?
5 Are there changes in the poem's rhythm? Where and why do these occur?

THE VOICE OF THE POEM

Each poem has its own voice. When you read a poet's work, you can often recognise a distinctive poetic voice. This may be in the poem's rhythms or in the viewpoint it expresses. Sometimes it is most evident in the tone of voice of the poem. Sometimes you are taken by the warmth of a poetic voice, or its coldness and detachment, or its tone of amused surprise. Try to catch the distinctive characteristic of the voice of the poem as you read. Decide if it is a man's voice or a woman's voice and what this might mean. Try to place the voice in a context. This may help you to understand the assumptions in the poem's statements, or the emotional force of those statements.

THE IMAGERY OF THE POEM

Images are the descriptive words and phrases used by poets to speak to our senses. They are mostly visual in quality (word pictures) but they can also appeal to our senses of touch, smell and hearing. Images and patterns of imagery are key elements in the way that poems convey meanings. They create moods, capture emotions and suggest or call out feelings in the readers.

Ask yourself these questions:
1 Are there patterns of images in the poem?
2 What kind of world is suggested by the images of the poem – familiar or strange, fertile or barren, secure or threatening, private or public, calm or stormy, generous or mean? (Images often suggest contrasts or opposites.)
3 What emotions are associated with the images of the poem?
4 What emotions, do you think, inspired the choice of images?
5 What emotions do the images cause in you?
6 If there are images which are particularly powerful, why do they carry the force they do?
7 Do any of the images have the force of a symbol?
8 What is the usual meaning of the symbol?
9 What is its meaning in the poem?

THE STRUCTURE OF THE POEM

There are endless possibilities for structuring a poem. The obvious structures of a poem are the lines and the stanzas. Short lines give a sense of tautness to a poem. Long lines can create a conversational feel and allow for shifts and changes in rhythm. Rhyme and the pattern of rhyme influence the structure of a poem.

The poem is also structured by the movement of thought. This may or may not coincide with line and stanza divisions. Words like 'while', 'then' and 'and' help you trace the line of thought or argument as it develops through the poem.

In narrative poems, a simple form of structure is provided by the story itself and the sequence of events it describes. Another simple structure is one in which the poet describes a scene and then records his/her response to it. Or a poem may be built on a comparison or a contrast. The structure may also come from a series of parallel statements or a series of linked reflections.

However, the structure of a poem can be quite subtle, dependent on such things as word association or changes in emotions. Be alert to a change of focus or a shift of thought or emotion in the poem. Quite often there is a creative tension between the stanza structure – the visual form of the poem – and the emotional or imaginative structure of the poem. For this reason, be alert to turning points in poems. These might be marked by a pause, by a change in imagery or by a variation in rhythm.

EXAM ADVICE FROM THE DEPARTMENT OF EDUCATION AND SCIENCE

The Department of Education and Science published this advice to students on answering the unseen poem in the Leaving Certificate Examination:

As the unseen poem on the paper will more than likely be unfamiliar to you, you should read it a number of times (at least twice) before attempting your answer. You should pay careful attention to the introductory note printed above the text of the poem.

Other advice from the Department of Education includes the following explanation of terms and questions, which are relevant to the answering of the questions on the unseen poem:

Do you agree with this statement?
You are free to agree in full or in part with the statement offered. But you must deal with the statement in question – you cannot simply dismiss the statement and write about a different topic of your choice.

Write a response to this statement (or Discuss)
As above, your answer can show the degree to which you agree or disagree with a statement or point of view. You can also deal with the impact the text made on you as a reader.

What does the poem say to you about …?
What is being asked for here is **your** understanding/reading of the poem. It is important that you show how your understanding comes from the text of the poem, its language and imagery.

LAST WORD

The really essential part in reading a poem is that you try to meet the poet halfway. Bring your intelligence and your emotions to the encounter with a poem and match the openness of the poet with an equal openness of mind and heart. And when you write about a poem, give your honest assessment.

GUIDELINES FOR ANSWERING QUESTIONS ON POETRY

Questions may be phrased in different ways in the Leaving Cert English exam. Some examples include:

- Do you like the poetry of Poet U?
- Poet V: a Personal Response.
- What impact did the poetry of Poet W have on you as a reader?
- Write an introduction to the poetry of Poet X.
- Compile a selection of the poems of Poet Y for an anthology, giving reasons for your choices.
- Give a short talk on the poetry of Poet Z.

Whatever way the question is phrased, you will need to show that you have engaged fully with the work of the poet under discussion.

FORMING A PERSONAL RESPONSE TO A POET'S THEMES

Each and every reader responds to a poem individually. It may be that the work of a particular poet moves us in ways that we can never hope to understand fully. But having said that, if your answer is to become more than just a series of vague impressions, there are aspects of a poet's work that you should consider in your answers. You must look closely at the poet's choice of **themes.** Illustrate them with examples but don't just write out a list of themes! Your answer should show that you have considered this aspect of the poet's work carefully. Questions you should ask yourself include:

- do you find the themes appealing because they reflect your personal concerns and interests?
- do the themes offer an insight into the life of the poet?
- do the themes enrich your understanding of universal human concerns, love or death, for example?
- do you respond to the poet's themes because they are unusual or unfamiliar?
- do you respond to themes that appeal to the intellect as well as the emotions, such as politics, religion or history, for example?

Bear in mind that themes may be complex and open to more than one interpretation. In fact this is often the aspect that we respond to most.

In your answer you should consider how the poet develops the themes, what questions are raised in your mind and how they may or may not be resolved.

THE POET'S LIFE, PERSONALITY OR OUTLOOK

Since poems are often written out of a poet's inner urgency, they can reveal a great deal about the personality of the poet:

- poems can be as revealing as an autobiography. Read the work of each of the poets carefully with this in mind. Can you build up a profile of each poet from what he or she has written, from his or her own personal voice?
- is this voice honest, convincing, suggesting an original or perceptive view of the world?
- it may also be that you like the work of a particular poet for a contrasting reason – that he or she goes beyond personal revelation to create other voices, other lives. Many poets adopt a different persona to recreate a particular experience. Might this enrich our understanding of the world? Your response may take this aspect into account, too.

THE POET'S USE OF LANGUAGE

Your response to a poet's work will be influenced by how he or she uses language. In your answer you should include an exploration of language.

In preparing for the examination you should examine carefully the individual **images** or **patterns of imagery** used by each of the eight poets on your course.

When you write about imagery, try to analyse how the particular poet you are dealing with creates the effects he or she does:

- does he or she appeal to our senses – our visual, tactile and aural senses, and our senses of taste and smell? How do you respond? Do you find the images effective in conveying theme or emotion?
- do the images appeal to you because their clarity and vividness allow you to visualise the scene or because they leave you baffled and puzzled in an exciting way?
- are the images created by the use of **simile** and **metaphor?** Can you say why these particular comparisons were chosen by the poet? Do you find them precise, surprising, fresh …?
- if the poet made use of **symbol** or **personification,** consider how these devices might have added to a poem's richness, so that it acquires a universal significance
- you may find you like the way a particular poet blends poetic and conversational language, or how a poet uses language both to **denote** (to signify) and to **connote** (to suggest).
- you may respond positively to a poet's simplicity of expression or to a sense that a poet's use of complex language reflects complex ideas.

An exploration of language may include style, manner, phraseology and vocabulary, as well as imagery and techniques mentioned above.

THE SOUNDS OF POETRY

Many people find that it is the sound of poetry that they respond to most. It is an ancient human characteristic to respond to word patterns like **rhyme** or musical effects such as **rhythm**. This may be one of the aspects of a particular poet's work that appeals to you most.

Poets use sound effects such as **alliteration, assonance, consonance** and **onomatopoeia** for many reasons – some thematic, some for emotive effect, some merely because of the sheer pleasure of creating pleasant musical word patterns.

Look carefully at how each of the poets you have studied makes use of sound. Your response will be much richer if based on close reading and attention to sound patterns and effects.

POETRY AND THE EMOTIONS

We may respond intellectually to the themes of a poem, but very often it is the emotional intensity of a poem that enables us to engage with it most fully. At their best, poems celebrate what it is to be human, with all that being human suggests, including confronting our deepest fears and anxieties.

The **tone** of a poem conveys the emotions that lie behind it. All of the elements in a poem may be used to convey tone and emotion. A poet's choice of imagery and the language he uses can be very expressive. Remember, too, that the use of sound conveys emotions well. Do look at the work of the different poets with this in mind.

What corresponding emotions does the work of each poet on your course create in you as a reader? Do you feel consoled, uplifted, disturbed, perhaps even alienated? Does the poet succeed in conveying his or her feelings, if indeed that is what is intended in the poem? These are questions you should consider in preparing to form your response.

CONCLUSION

It is worth remembering that you will be rewarded for your attempts to come to terms with the work of the poets you have studied in a personal and responsive way. This may entail a heartfelt negative response, too. But even a negative response must display close reading and should pay attention to specific aspects of the poems. Do not feel that you have to conform to the opinions of others – including the opinions expressed in this book!

Read each question carefully. Some questions may direct your attention to specific elements of a poet's work. Make sure you deal with these in your answer. Other questions may simply invite you to include some aspects of a poet's work in your response. It would be unwise to ignore any hints as to how to proceed!

You will be required to support your answer by reference to or quotation from the poems chosen. Remember that long quotations are hardly ever necessary.

The Department of Education and Science has published the following advice to students on answering the question on poetry:

It is a matter of judgement as to which of the poems will best suit the question under discussion and candidates should not feel a necessity to refer to all of the poems they have studied.

As in all of the questions in the examination, you will be marked using the following criteria:

1 *Clarity of purpose (30% of marks available)* This is explained by the Department of Education and Science as 'engagement with the set task' – in other words, are you answering the question you have been asked? Is your answer relevant and focused?

2 *Coherence of delivery (30% of marks available)* Here you are assessed on your 'ability to sustain the response over the entire answer'. Is there coherence and continuity in the points you are making? Are the references you choose to illustrate your points appropriate?

3 *Efficiency of language use (30% of marks available)* The Department of Education and Science explains this as the 'management and control of language to achieve clear communication'. Aspects of your writing such as vocabulary, use of phrasing, and fluency – your writing style – will be taken into account.

4 *Accuracy of mechanics (10% of marks available)* Your levels of accuracy in spelling and grammar are what count here. Always leave some time during the exam to read over your work – you are bound to spot errors.

Good luck!

GLOSSARY
OF TERMS

ALLITERATION

This is a figure of speech in which consonants, especially at the beginning of words, are repeated. The term itself means 'repeating and playing upon the same letter'. Alliteration is a common feature of poetry in every period of literary history. It is used mainly for emphasis, to reinforce a point. A good example is found in John Donnes's sonnet 'Batter My Heart', where the speaker asks God to 'bend / Your force, to break, blowe, burn, and make me new'. Robert Frost uses alliteration in his poem 'Birches': 'When I see birches bend to left and right'.

ALLUSION

An allusion is a reference to a person, place or event or to another work of art or literature. The purpose of allusion is to get the reader to share an experience which has significant meaning for the writer. When a writer makes use of allusion, he or she takes it for granted that the reader will possess the background knowledge necessary to understand its significance in the context of the work. In many cases, the significance of the allusion becomes clearer as the poem evolves. The title of Elizabeth Bishop's poem 'The Prodigal' is an allusion to Christ's parable of the prodigal son told in the Gospel of St Luke. The poem alludes to some of the themes of that parable.

AMBIGUITY

Ambiguous words, phrases or sentences are capable of being understood in two or more possible senses. In many poems, ambiguity is part of the poet's method and is essential to the meaning of the poem. The tile of Philip Larkin's poem 'Church Going' involves a suggestive ambiguity. It means both 'going to church' and 'the church going' (i.e. disappearing, going out of use, or becoming decayed).

ASSONANCE

This is the repetition of identical or similar vowel sounds, especially in stressed syllables, in a sequence of nearby words. Assonance can contribute significantly to the meaning of a poem. An example is 'That night the slow sea washed against my head' from Derek Mahon's 'Day Trip to Donegal'.

BALLAD

Ballads were originally songs, transmitted orally. They commented on life by telling stories in a popular style. In ballads, the attention of the readers is concentrated on the story and the characters. Every ballad must have a meaning that can easily be grasped by the reader. 'Sir Patrick Spens' is one of the most celebrated of all ballads. Its first two stanzas exemplify the main features found in almost all ballads: the abrupt and arresting opening, the economical sketch of the setting and action and the sharp transition from narrative to dialogue and back again. Other features of ballads are refrains, repetitions and simplicity of diction.

COLLOQUIALISM

A colloquial word or phrase is one that is used in everyday speech and writing. The colloquial style is plain and relaxed. At the end of the eighteenth century, Wordsworth declared that his aim was to imitate, as far as possible, what he called 'the very language of men'. In much poetry of the twentieth and twenty-first centuries, there is an acceptance of colloquialism, even slang, as a medium of poetic expression. The poems of Philip Larkin frequently exemplify this idea.

CONCEIT

The term 'conceit' is generally used for figures of speech that establish arresting parallels between objects or situations which, at first glance, seem to have little or nothing in common. All comparisons discover a likeness in things unalike. A comparison becomes a conceit when the poet forces us to concede likeness, while at the same time we are strongly conscious of unlikeness. The conceit is a characteristic device of the seventeenth-century metaphysical poets, among them

Donne and Herbert. Sometimes an entire poem can be a long conceit. An example is Donne's 'The Anniversarie', which consists of a series of comparisons and contrasts between two lovers and two royal persons.

CONVENTION

This is the name given to any aspect of a literary work which author and readers accept as normal and to be expected in that kind of writing. For example, it is a convention that a sonnet has fourteen lines that rhyme in a certain pattern. By convention, the ballad has a particular kind of diction. Sometimes conventions are abandoned or replaced. Eighteenth-century poetic diction, for example, gave way to a more 'natural' form of expression.

DICTION

Diction is the vocabulary used by a writer – his or her selection of words. Until the beginning of the nineteenth century, poets wrote in accordance with the principle that the diction of poetry had to differ, often significantly, from that of current speech. There was, in other words, a certain sort of 'poetic' diction which, by avoiding commonplace words and expressions, was supposed to lend dignity to the poem and its subject. This is entirely contrary to modern practice.

GENRE

The term is used to signify a particular literary species or form. Traditionally, the important genres were epic, tragedy, comedy, elegy, satire, lyric and pastoral. Until modern times, critics tended to distinguish carefully between the various genres and writers were expected to follow the rules prescribed for each. For example, if a poet wrote an epic, it was assumed that his or her language would be dignified, in keeping with the heroic nature of the subject, and that he or she would use epic similes, often many lines in length. Epics were also expected to feature long descriptive passages.

IMAGERY

This is a term with a very wide application. When we speak of the imagery of a poem, we refer to all its images taken collectively. The poet C. Day Lewis puts the matter well when he describes an image as 'a picture made out of words'. If we consider imagery in its narrow and popular sense, it signifies descriptions of visible objects and scenes, as, for example, in Robert Frost's 'Birches' the trees are 'Loaded with ice a sunny winter morning'. In its wider sense, imagery signifies figurative language, especially metaphor and simile.

LYRIC

Originally a lyric was a song performed to the accompaniment of a lyre. The term is now used to signify any relatively short poem in which a single speaker, not necessarily representing the poet, expresses feelings and thoughts in a personal and subjective fashion. Most poems are either lyrics or feature large lyrical elements.

METAPHOR AND SIMILE

These are the two commonest figures of speech in poetry. A simile contains two parts – a subject that is the focus of attention, and another element that is introduced for the sake of emphasising some quality in the subject. In a simile, the poet uses some such word as 'like' or 'as' to show that a comparison is being made. The opening lines of Sylvia Plath's 'Finisterre' feature a striking metaphor: 'This was the land's end: the last fingers, knuckled and rheumatic, / Cramped on nothing'.

Metaphor differs from simile only in omitting the comparative word ('like' or 'as'). If in a simile someone's teeth are like pearls, in a metaphor they *are* pearls. While in the case of a simile the comparison is openly proclaimed as such, in the case of a metaphor the comparison is implied. A metaphor is capable of a greater range of suggestiveness than a simile and its implications are wider and richer. The simile, by its very nature (with the 'like' or 'as' formula), is limited to a comparatively small area of suggestion. One advantage of metaphor is its tendency to establish numerous relationships between the two things being compared. In John Montague's 'Windharp', the poet imagines a hand combing and stroking the landscape 'till / the valley gleams / like the pile upon / a mountain pony's coat'.

ONOMATOPOEIA

This involves the use of words that resemble, or enact, the very sounds they imitate. If a poet tries to make the sound reflect the meaning, he or she is using onomatopoeia. In 'The War Horse', Eavan Boland uses a simple form of onomatopoeia when she writes about the 'the clip, clop casual / iron' of the horse's shoes.

PARADOX

This is an apparently self-contradictory statement which, on further consideration, is found to contain an essential truth. Paradox is so intrinsic to human nature that poetry rich in paradox is valued as a reflection of the central truths of human experience. John Donne is one of the great masters of paradox. In his sonnet 'Batter My Heart', he is addressing God in a series of paradoxical demands: 'Take mee to you, imprison mee, for I / Except you enthrall mee, never shall be free'.

SIMILE

See 'metaphor and simile'.

SONNET

This is a single-stanza lyric, consisting of fourteen lines. These fourteen lines are just long enough to make possible the fairly complex development of a single theme, and short enough to test the poet's gift for concentrated expression. The poet's freedom is further restricted by a demanding rhyme scheme and a conventional metrical form (five strong stresses in each line). The greatest sonnets are those in which the poet has overcome the limitations of the form and achieved the great aim of reconciling freedom of expression, variety of rhythm, mood and tone and richness of imagery with adherence to a rigid set of conventions.

English poets have traditionally written one of two kinds of sonnet – the Petrarchan and the Shakespearean. The Petrarchan sonnet, favoured by Milton and Wordsworth, falls into two divisions – the octave (eight lines rhyming abba, abba) and the sestet (six lines generally rhyming cde, cde). The octave generally presents a problem, situation or incident; the sestet resolves the problem or comments on the situation or incident. In contrast, the Shakespearean sonnet consists of three quatrains (groups of four lines rhyming abab, cdcd, efef) and a rhyming couplet (gg).

STYLE

This may be defined as the manner of expression characteristic of a writer – that is, his or her particular way of saying things. Consideration of style involves an examination of the writer's diction, figures of speech, order of words, tone and feeling, rhythm and movement. Traditionally, styles were classified according to three categories: high (formal or learned), middle and low (plain). Convention required that the level of style be appropriate to the speaker, the subject matter, the occasion which inspired the poem and the literary genre. A modern critic, Northrop Frye, suggests that styles could be classified under two broad headings: (a) demotic style, modelled on the language, rhythms and associations of everyday speech, and (b) hieratic style, involving formal, elaborate expression, with the aim of separating literary language from ordinary speech.

SYMBOL

A symbol is anything that stands for something else. In this sense, all words are symbols because they signify things other than themselves. Literary symbolism, however, comes about when the *objects* signified by the words stand in turn for things other than themselves. At a simple level, symbolism is familiar to almost everybody because certain conventional symbols are universally popular. Objects commonly associated with fixed ideas or qualities have come to symbolise these: for example, the cross is the primary Christian symbol, and the dove is a symbol of peace. Colour symbols have no fixed meaning, but derive their significance from a context: green may signify innocence or Irish patriotism or envy. The literary symbol is not a token with a precise meaning to be pinned down and accurately described. Some poets use symbols as essentially private tokens so that even the context can do little to help them to generate their meanings. When Yeats, for example, does this, he sets his readers some difficult problems of interpretation. In John Montague's poem on his father, the cage inside which the latter works, as well as being an actual place, is also symbolic – not only of the father's trapped existence, but of the human condition in general. Montague is suggesting that we are all captives in cages, whether these are our own weaknesses, our own bodies, or the societies which make us prisoners of the convictions they impose.

TONE

When one is trying to describe the tone of a poem, it is best to think of every poem as a spoken, rather than a written, exercise. A poem has at least one speaker who is addressing somebody or something. In some poems, the speaker can be thought of as meditating aloud, talking to himself or herself. We, the readers, catch him or her in the act and overhear them. Every speaker must inevitably have an attitude to the person or object being addressed or talked about, and must also see himself or herself in some relationship with that person or object. This attitude or relationship will determine the tone of the utterance. Tone may thus be defined as the expression of a literary speaker's attitude to, and relationship with, the listener or the subject. In real life, a person's attitude to another is often revealed in the tone of voice of that person and in the words chosen. A sensitive reading aloud of most poems will soon reveal the tone of a speaker's utterance. Philip Larkin's poems present an interesting study in tone. He approaches his subject-matter in a matter-of-fact way, and this is reflected in the casual, unpretentious tone.

18538216